By the same author

Land of France (*with Lord Holden*)
The English Country House
The English Garden
The English Interior
Wessex
The Age of Wren
London Homes
Normandy and Brittany
The Victorian Home
The Châteaux of France
English Court Life
Hinton Ampner: A Hampshire Manor

HAMPSHIRE

1 (overleaf) *Swan Green, in the New Forest*

RALPH DUTTON

HAMPSHIRE

B. T. BATSFORD LTD

LONDON

First published 1970

Text printed in Great Britain by Northumberland Press Ltd, Gateshead, Co. Durham. Plates printed and books bound by Richard Clay (The Chaucer Press) Ltd, Bungay, Suffolk, for the publishers B. T. Batsford Ltd, 4 Fitzhardinge Street, London W 1

SBN 7134 0065 X

CONTENTS

ILLUSTRATIONS

The plates are reproduced by kind permission of the following: Noel Habgood—1, 13, 26; Kenneth Scowen—2, 8, 9, 27, 28; Peter Baker—3, 14, 36; Edwin Smith—4-7, 11, 12, 16, 18, 19, 22; Louis and Daphne Peek—10; A. F. Kersting—15, 17, 20, 21, 23-25, 29-34; Thomas A. Wilkie—35. The jacket illustration, of Selborne, is by Kenneth Scowen.

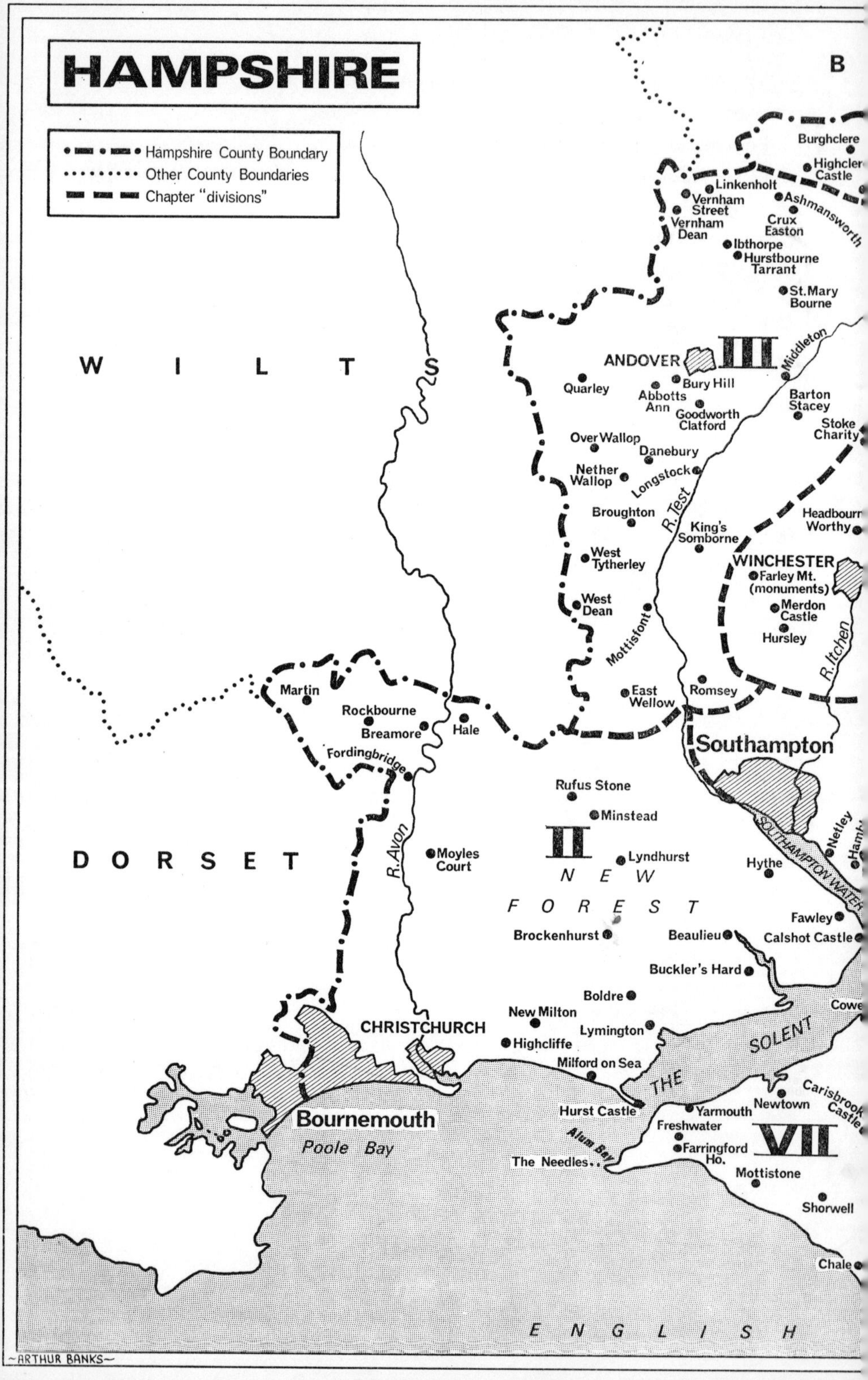

HAMPSHIRE
Hampshire County Boundary
Other County Boundaries
Chapter "divisions"
B
W I L T S
D O R S E T
Burghclere
Highclere Castle
Linkenholt
Vernham Street
Vernham Dean
Ashmansworth
Crux Easton
Ibthorpe
Hurstbourne Tarrant
St. Mary Bourne
III
ANDOVER
Middleton
Bury Hill
Quarley
Abbotts Ann
Goodworth Clatford
Barton Stacey
Stoke Charity
Over Wallop
Danebury
Nether Wallop
Longstock
R. Test
Broughton
King's Somborne
Headbourne Worthy
West Tytherley
WINCHESTER
Farley Mt. (monuments)
Merdon Castle
Hursley
West Dean
Mottisfont
R. Itchen
Martin
Rockbourne
Breamore
Hale
East Wellow
Romsey
Fordingbridge
Southampton
Rufus Stone
Minstead
II
Moyles Court
R. Avon
Lyndhurst
N E W
F O R E S T
Hythe
SOUTHAMPTON WATER
Netley
Fawley
Brockenhurst
Beaulieu
Calshot Castle
Buckler's Hard
Boldre
New Milton
CHRISTCHURCH
Lymington
Highcliffe
Milford on Sea
THE SOLENT
Cowes
Bournemouth
Poole Bay
Hurst Castle
Yarmouth
Newtown
Carisbrooke Castle
Freshwater
Alum Bay
Farringford Ho.
VII
The Needles
Mottistone
Shorwell
Chale
E N G L I S H
~ARTHUR BANKS~

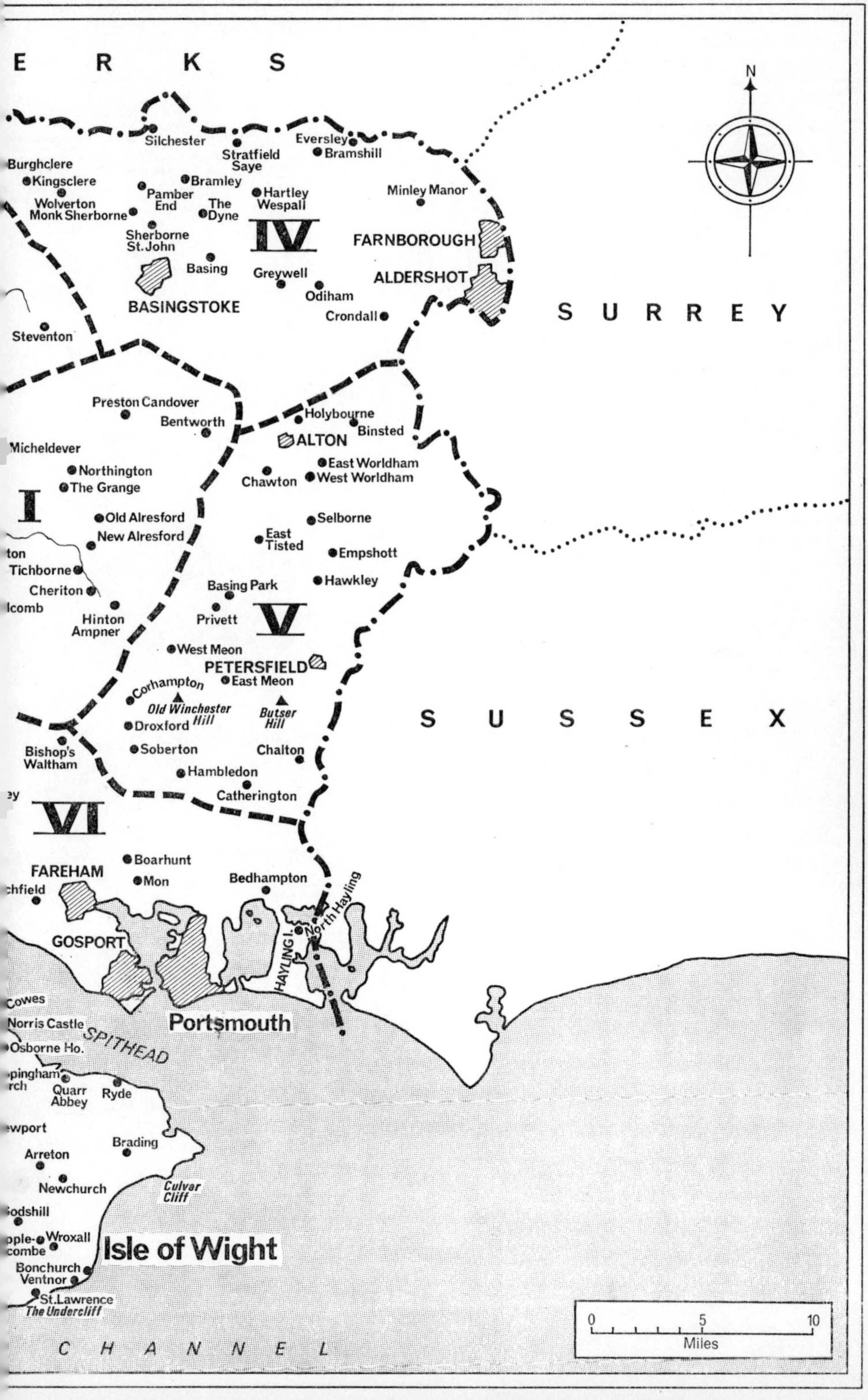

ERKS
Silchester
Stratfield Saye
Eversley
Bramshill
Burghclere
Kingsclere
Bramley
Pamber End
Hartley Wespall
Minley Manor
Wolverton
Monk Sherborne
The Dyne
IV
FARNBOROUGH
Sherborne St. John
Basing
Greywell
ALDERSHOT
Odiham
BASINGSTOKE
Crondall
SURREY
Steventon
Preston Candover
Bentworth
Holybourne
Binsted
ALTON
Micheldever
East Worldham
Northington
Chawton
West Worldham
The Grange
I
Old Alresford
Selborne
New Alresford
East Tisted
Empshott
ton
Tichborne
Hawkley
Cheriton
Basing Park
lcomb
V
Hinton Ampner
Privett
West Meon
PETERSFIELD
East Meon
Corhampton
Old Winchester Hill
Butser Hill
SUSSEX
Droxford
Soberton
Chalton
Bishop's Waltham
Hambledon
Catherington
ey
VI
Boarhunt
FAREHAM
Mon
Bedhampton
chfield
North Hayling
GOSPORT
HAYLING I.
Cowes
Norris Castle
Portsmouth
SPITHEAD
Osborne Ho.
pingham
rch
Quarr Abbey
Ryde
ewport
Brading
Arreton
Newchurch
Culver Cliff
Godshill
Wroxall
pple-
combe
Isle of Wight
Bonchurch
Ventnor
St.Lawrence
The Undercliff
CHANNEL
0
5
10
Miles
N

Introduction

The writer of a readable guidebook should possess, I think, a comprehensive knowledge of a wide range of subjects. He should be able to write in an authoritative manner about palaeology, geology, history through the centuries, architecture both ecclesiastical and domestic, agriculture, and forestry. He should be able to show culture by reference to the literary figures who have lived in the area under review, he should show an appreciation of landscape and other aspects of the countryside; and all this information should be welded into a graceful prose.

Few of us, I fear, attain these heights, and I must in truthfulness admit that there are a number of chinks in my armour of knowledge and that in some of these subjects I by no means reach A level. Prehistory, I fear, is one of them. I can lead the reader to a Bronze Age fort, but once having arrived on the scene I must leave him to make his own deductions. In geology, too, my knowledge is far from profound, indeed I find it a somewhat dry subject. My interest lies only in the effect the subsoil has on the surface of the ground, on the contours, on the trees and plants, and generally on the landscape.

I make this little confession so that the reader may not feel that he has caught me out in a pretention to a greater erudition than I in fact possess. However, in spite of shortcomings I propose to plunge ahead for better or for worse.

I suppose we all form a mental picture of counties with which we have only a superficial acquaintance, a picture which is immediately brought to mind by the name of the county. I know that to me Sussex suggests a fertile, well-treed landscape with downs rising beyond woodlands, and Wiltshire a contrast of rolling barren hills and deep leafy valleys, while Surrey and Berkshire conjure up rather unattractive pictures—which I know to be unjust, for they both contain some areas of great beauty.

Following this line of thought, I have often wondered what the name Hampshire suggests to those that know the county very little. To many, I suppose, it is merely a region through which one passes to reach more romantic country further west. The hurrying motorist on the road from London enters the county west of Camberley, crosses the sandy desolation of Hartford Bridge Flats, passes industrial Basingstoke, and so over the bleak area of High Hampshire to Andover with all the hurly-burly of a vastly expanding town and new roads cut through the solid chalk of the subsoil. Or perhaps he follows the south road from Sussex and almost as soon as he comes into Hampshire passes through mile upon mile of urbanisation, either intense or desultory, until his road reaches the area of the New Forest two thirds of the way across the county and some miles beyond Southampton. But the relief is only temporary: he soon finds himself once again amongst the bricks and mortar of Christchurch and Bournemouth.

What picture of Hampshire can the motorist following either of these two routes obtain, what impression can he carry away of this ancient county? It can hardly be very favourable. Yet away from trunk roads there are vast areas of tranquil, gentle landscape with villages lying amongst the undulations and surrounded by deep woodlands and arable fields. There is little that can impress by grandeur or unusual loveliness of scenery, although the downs on the east and in the north rise to fairly dramatic heights, and the valleys of the Itchen and the Test have stretches of great beauty. But on the whole Hampshire does not boast a landscape which calls for superlatives, and it is rather the intimate, unpretentious charm of the countryside and its small towns and villages which ensures for it a high place amongst the attractive counties of England.

I think, too, that there is a certain reticence about Hampshire which endears it to those that know it well. Like a person with a reserved character, it reveals its graces only on close acquaintance, and a passing traveller may have a brief contact without discovering the charm and interest which are concealed beneath a rather stern exterior. It is a county which has inspired great affection in those who have known it well, and one thinks immediately of a writer such as Gilbert White who spent the greater part of his life so happily and industriously living at the foot of the steep, beech-covered hangers of Selborne and seeing so much with his observant eye that was hidden to the ordinary man. Or William Cobbett, a much more peripatetic and violent character, who was continually returning to Hampshire to admire its natural beauties and to castigate many of its landowners.

It is an affection which survives still amongst many of its inhabitants, but for how long, one wonders, will the county be allowed to retain the quiet beauty which is so appealing? No county lies under so great a threat of destruction. In the north there are the hugely expanding towns of Basingstoke and Andover, in the south the unification and extension northward of Southampton and Portsmouth, forming what is sometimes called the Solent City—though this name is not popular with the planners, who prefer to call it 'large-scale development', designed to accommodate 60,000 Londoners. But this is not all: a scheme has been devised for development northward up the Itchen valley past Winchester, which would presumably be engulfed, as far as Stoke Charity, now a sequestered little hamlet. How far these progressive schemes will eventually be implemented it is impossible to say, but if they are, there will be little left of rural Hampshire except the chalk area to the east of Winchester, and the New Forest. This is a gloomy picture, but not perhaps more gloomy than the reality; the fact that at least some of this projected development cannot anyhow materialise for some years to come is small consolation.

A guidebook, even a discursive book such as this, should, I think, provide a few hard facts and figures for the enquiring reader. Hampshire, then, with the Isle of Wight which is part of the shire proper, covers an area of 1,661 square miles and, with the Isle, has nearly 200 miles of coastline. It exceeds the size of Sussex by a little over 200 square miles, and Wiltshire by more than 300 square miles. These large figures mean little to most of us, and a more easily comprehensible measure is the length of a diagonal line drawn across the county from north-east to south-west, approximately from Farnborough to Bournemouth, which is 65 miles. This, since the county is roughly rectangular, gives a good idea of its scale.

The boundaries of the county, much as they are now, came into being at a very early date. In the last quarter of the sixth century Cerdic and his Saxons invaded south Britain and conquered the country extending from the river Arun on the east to the Avon on the west, thus securing the area adjoining that already subdued by the South Saxons beyond the Arun. This was the beginning of the Kingdom of Wessex, which two and a half centuries later was destined to control the whole of England south of the Tweed.

The eastern boundary of Wessex moved soon after its formation to the little river Ems, where the boundary of the shire still remains, while on the north the rivers Enborne and Blackwater formed a practical frontier. On the west the boundary remained more fluid and fluctuated with the varying strength of Wessex, and there are no particular natural features for its eventual fixture to the west of the valley of the Avon. Indeed so complex remained stretches of the boundary about halfway along its course, with pockets of Wiltshire enclosed in Hampshire, that in 1895 a new boundary was drawn in this area which included in Hampshire the parishes of South Damerham, Martin, and Whitbury, which had previously formed part of Wiltshire, thus creating a smoother outline, but forming what is known as 'the Martin peninsula' which projects rather strangely into Wiltshire only five miles south of Salisbury.

The capital of the Kingdom of Wessex was, of course, Winchester, the Saxons thus making use of the fortified town which the Romans had built at the strategic point where the river Itchen passes through the long chain of downs which runs east and west across the centre of the county. On the analogy of several other counties it might well have been expected that Hampshire would have received a name such as Wintonshire, thus making it the shire of its central town. But when the shires were created in the first half of the seventh century—and Hampshire was one of the earliest created—the importance of Winchester had been for many years on the decline, while Southampton, a safe and in every way admirable port, had

2 *East Meon church*

become the major town of the region. Thus as the County of Southampton, Hampshire makes its first recorded appearance in the *Anglo-Saxon Chronicle* of 755; and thus, too, its official name remained until 20 years or so ago, when this ancient but cumbersome nomenclature was dropped for the more practical name of Hampshire.

Some nineteenth-century authors attributed the name of the town and hence of the whole county to the river Anton, which has a short and inglorious course before joining the river Test a few miles south of Andover. The theory being that after this marriage the Test adopted the name of its smaller partner and since the combined waters flowed into salt water at the apex of what is now Southampton Water it provided a name for the port which grew up close to its mouth. It was an engaging but fallacious theory, for in fact the name Southampton is derived very simply from the Saxon Hamtun, *Tun* meaning a village and *Ham* land by a river.

The decline of Winchester before the increasing importance of Southampton was not permanent. Within a century of the latter providing a name for the county, Winchester was not only once again the most important town in the shire, but was also the capital of the Kingdom of Wessex, and thus it was to remain during the many invasions and vicissitudes of the following centuries. As the rulers of Wessex became the rulers of all England, so Winchester became the civil capital of the country, a proud position it finally lost under the Plantagenets. In 1194 Richard Coeur de Lion was crowned in Winchester, the ceremony being designed to obliterate the disgrace of the year of captivity he had suffered in the hands of the Emperor Henry VI as he returned from his brilliant crusade. But already for some time Winchester had been fighting a losing battle against London as the administrative capital of England, and only the fact that the King's Treasury was kept in the city gave support to the claim of precedence for Winchester, a claim which the leading citizens never failed to press, though usually unsuccessfully, at the great ceremonies of state. Although Winchester was to receive many marks of special royal favour during following reigns, these were compliments rather to its former than to its actual importance.

3 *Lymington: Georgian façades in Quay Hill*

Introduction

Almost every English county contains within its bounds landscape of great variety, but in Hampshire topography varies more than in most, or so it seems to me—but perhaps it is merely that, since I have known this county all my life, I distinguish subtleties of change more distinctly than elsewhere. The Frenchman who wrote of '*cette terrible verdure anglaise*' and complained that the landscape of England lacked all variety may seem to us to have been obtuse; and yet there may be something in his point of view. If one were suddenly deposited in England one could probably guess where one was, one would know that one was not in a country large in scale like France, of the flatness of Holland, or in the fierce countryside of Spain. So perhaps England has some overall quality which to a casual observer produces a character of sameness, and that it is only to the inhabitants that it appears so agreeably diverse.

This applies in a more restricted sense to counties, and it is to dispel this impression that I endeavour in the following pages to show the change of landscape and physical features which occur in Hampshire. The alterations are created, of course, by the soil, which changes distinctly and suddenly in different parts of the county; the rolling, rather austere country with a chalk subsoil of the central heart gives way abruptly to north and south to the flatter clay country with its more crowded aspect of small fields and much hedgerow timber. In the extreme north-east and south-west are areas of sour sand unable to support anything more attractive than indifferent pine trees, while parallel to the eastern boundary runs a narrow belt of upper greensand which with its attendant strata gives rise to the long line of quite sensational cliff-like hangers.

In fact the purpose of this little book is to present a picture of the county as a whole with towns and villages in their landscape setting without dwelling exclusively on architectural features. I have not hesitated to be selective and discursive rather than exhaustive, and I lead the patient reader to places I myself find interesting or attractive—indeed, how else is one to arrive at the principle of selectivity without relying on one's own preferences?—and here and there I enlarge on personalities of the past, mostly authors whose writings bring one in touch with the county at their time.

Just as Hampshire is not in general a county of great scenery, so too, it is not a county of great architecture, either ecclesiastical or domestic. In Winchester, of course, it has a cathedral whose interior, at least to my prejudiced eye, is as splendid as any in the world, whilst the robust Norman walls of Romsey Abbey can vie with any in the country, and few villages have a parish church as noble as East Meon. But these are exceptions, and on the whole parish churches have little of the grandeur of those in the limestone areas, and it would seem that Hampshire was not a rich county in mediaeval days, and that the soil did not provide the prosperity for landowners which would have led to the raising of magnificent edifices to the glory of God.

For the same reason, presumably, there are few country houses of the highest architectural importance in the county. There are in fact only three in this category which are regularly open to the public: The Vyne, Mottisfont, and Breamore. Bramshill, which would be outstanding in any county, is now a police college and so is not available. These four houses are all near the edge of the county, and such large houses as are—or were—in the central region (The Grange, near Alresford, and Hursley for example) were the product of nineteenth- or twentieth-century affluence which did not stem from the land.

There are, of course, a number of others of interest, but it has seemed to me that in the following pages there is little advantage to the reader in my going into ecstasies over houses which are hidden from the public eye beyond belts of trees and park gates, so they have received only cursory references. But in Hampshire there are many good gardens surrounding the smaller country houses, of which there are a great number in the county, and many of these are open to the public on various days during each summer; the dates can be found in the booklet produced by the National Gardens Scheme, or in the pages of the county press. The high standard of the gardens is something of a triumph over natural conditions, for Hampshire in general is by no means an area where 'anything will grow'. But I think that perhaps the struggle to form a good garden on an indifferent soil or in a frost area leads to a more interesting or at least more individual garden than one produced in a place where all is favourable. Anyhow, I like to comfort myself with these sentiments in my own efforts.

If, then, neither the parish churches nor the country houses of Hampshire are in general of the highest order, I believe that some of the small towns would be outstanding for their charm in any county. Alresford, Fareham, Lymington, Odiham, Wickham (I place them in alphabetical order to show no favouritism), all have exceptional character and beauty, and all depend for their distinction on the trim eighteenth-century elevations they present to the streets, though many of these bland and comfortable façades conceal bodies of an earlier date. It is curious that English towns usually appear to have developed on different lines to those on the Continent. The latter are seldom laid out without a central square from which roads radiate into the countryside. This is rare in this country; there are exceptions in Hampshire of course—Petersfield for example—but of the four towns I have mentioned only Wickham can be said to have a central square, and even here the lines are not exactly Continental.

Of the large towns few, except Winchester, have much beauty. Portsmouth, in the Old High Street, had formerly one of the most fascinating streets in the county, with seventeenth-, eighteenth- and nineteenth-century buildings adjoining each other with perfect compatibility, but since the terrible destruction caused by war the charm has largely disappeared and the town must depend on its massive fortifications for its architectural interest. Much the same must be said of Southampton, but here not only the town walls survived but also two of its most interesting antiquities, the Bar Gate and the Tudor House. The other large towns, Basingstoke, Andover, Bournemouth, have not very much to attract those in search of interesting architecture, although the last has some contemporary buildings of distinction, and for this reason they have not received great attention in the following pages.

There are very few towns, however, which are entirely devoid of some feature of interest, and to those unwilling to miss any building of note I would like highly to recommend Professor Pevsner and

Mr David Lloyd's Penguin on Hampshire and the Isle of Wight. Although in size it is not quite for the pocket, it is certainly for the car, and it covers in detail every town and village in the county. I would like here to record my indebtedness to it, and also to the *Victoria County History*, published before the First World War, the five stout and heavy volumes of which are a mine of learned information; but this is not even for the car unless one happens to be travelling in a pantechnicon.

There are of course many other books on Hampshire published during this and past centuries, but my purpose in adding to the number is to produce a general survey without too much detail of the county of Hampshire, a county in which I was born, and in which I am fortunate enough still to live.

CHAPTER ONE

Winchester and the Itchen valley

The county of Hampshire is highly favoured in the position of its capital. Some counties—Oxfordshire and Wiltshire for example—have their capitals close to the county boundaries, and this must lead to considerable administrative difficulties; but the City of Winchester is set squarely in the centre of the county, almost exactly halfway between the greatest extremities. The distance from Winchester to Aldershot in the north-east corner of the county is approximately 30 miles as the crow flies, while to Bournemouth in the extreme south-west the distance covered by the same energetic bird is about five miles more. North to south, Winchester is equally well placed: the line where Hampshire gives away to Berkshire is about 22 miles distant, while Portsmouth, on the south coast of the county, is no more than 24 miles away.

This convenience of position is, of course, no more than a happy chance. The Belgae, who were presumably Celts, founded their settlement, which came to be known as Venta Belgarum, in this deep valley, where the river Itchen drives its way through the ridge of chalk hills, as a site where they could control the valley leading down to the sea. It was natural that the Romans with their keen sense of siting, both from the point of view of security and amenity, should have decided to make Venta Belgarum one of their principal towns in this area.

Although the Romans under Julius Caesar had first invaded Britain as early as 55 BC, their conquests had been confined to the south-east part of the country. But during the reign of Claudius, about 90 years later, the area which is now Hampshire came completely under Roman domination: the invading legions under the leadership of Vespasian, the future emperor, made Venta Belgarum, in the centre, and Calleva Atrebatum (later known as Silchester), in the north, the two principal towns of the area.

The Celtic settlement which the Romans found so happily placed in the well-watered valley between the hills was soon developed on the usual lines. The general form was a rectangle intersected with a grid of streets of which two were main thoroughfares, one from east to west, and the other north to south. This is the layout of the central part of Winchester which still survives. The whole was surrounded by a wall with gates opening to their new roads which streaked away across the uplands and valleys to the various important settlements in their colony.

In the City itself, only the layout of streets remains on the surface as a memorial of the Roman occupation, for the level of the ground has risen by 12 feet in the course of 1,900 years and only by excavation can evidence of this early civilisation be found. Naturally this is seldom a practical operation, but on several occasions, when buildings have been demolished, it has been possible to dig down to the level of the Roman town, and the remains of domestic structures have been found. Much must remain for ever buried under existing buildings.

If the town of the Romans has practically disappeared, their roads survive, and still form the basis for many of the principal highways leading away from Winchester. Like the spokes of a wheel radiating from the hub, the roads of central Hampshire spread a geometrical network over the countryside: to the south, a road led to Clausentum (now Bittern), a fortified post where the Itchen flows into Southampton Water; to the south-east to Porchester on its promontory jutting into the western of the three almost land-locked harbours of the southern seaboard. To the east, surprisingly enough, no road was made, or perhaps was begun and never completed, for the present road to Guildford, once it has negotiated the steep slope of St Giles' Hill, sets out with a Roman purposefulness towards the east but after a few miles loses its undeviating character and winds with the contours of the landscape like any non-Roman road. To the north-east an undeviating highway was laid to Calleva Atrebatum (Silchester), thus joining the two most important towns in the area, and this still forms the main London road via Basingstoke. Up and down hill it goes, straight as an arrow. This was no doubt most convenient for Roman chariots, but with its unexpected rises and falls it was, until recent improvements, one of the most dangerous roads in the county for cars.

To the north-west the spoke-like plan continues with a road sailing away over the Hampshire uplands 70 miles or so to Cirencester, while to the south of it, running almost due east to west, was the road to Old Sarum on its circular hill a couple of miles north of its later supplanter, Salisbury, in the valley of the Avon. Thus Winchester was strategically connected with all the principal settlements in the southern part of Britain, and had the Roman occupation continued for longer more evidence of their works would have embellished Hampshire. But in about AD 410 the Roman garrisons were withdrawn in order to defend their own country against the determined attacks of the Goths.

Edward Gibbon in *The Decline and Fall of the Roman Empire* devotes a passage to this rather obscure period in the history of this country: 'The regular forces, which guarded that remote province, had been gradually withdrawn; and Britain was abandoned, without defence, to the Saxon pirates, and the savages of Ireland and Caledonia.' He goes on to explain that the country was particularly vulnerable to invasion since under Roman rule each town in Britain —there were 92—was a self-governing republic, so that there was no united force to repel invaders.

Almost two centuries passed before St Augustine landed in England in 596, and with the spread of Christianity Winchester, which had been reduced to little more than a Saxon fort, began once again to become the important town it had been under the Romans, and to replace Southampton, which had superseded it, as the capital of Wessex. More than a century was still to pass before we reach the more tangible period in the history of Winchester when Alfred became King of Wessex. He succeeded to the crown in 871 and to a kingdom almost overrun by the Danes. The West Saxons, who had by this time formed a united people, after severe reverses eventually drove the Danes to the north of the Thames, and Alfred was able to develop his Kingdom of Wessex in comparative peace.

By this time the name Venta Belgarum had developed almost into its present form, for in the previous century it was mentioned by the Venerable Bede as Vintanceastir. It appears thus in his remarkable *Historia Ecclesiastica Gentis Anglorum*, which traces the ancient history of England down to the year AD 731. The five books of this tremendous work were translated into English by order of Alfred—one of the indications of the interest this remarkable man took in the history and culture of his country.

King Alfred is indeed the greatest figure in the history of Winchester, and it is sad that the exact burial place of his bones has now been lost. His body was first placed in the New Minster, which was begun after his death close to the site of the present cathedral. When this structure was demolished his body was removed to Hyde Abbey, just outside the north wall of the City. At the Dissolution the abbey was largely demolished and the resting place of Alfred's bones was lost.

It is fitting that a massive bronze statue, by Hamo Thornycroft, should be one of the first sights to meet the eye of a traveller on crossing the stone bridge over the Itchen from the east and entering the ancient confines of the City. It is the rear view of this illustrious personage, certainly, for he faces westward from his high granite plinth across the Broadway, which is flanked on the south side by the nineteenth-century Gothic Guildhall, to the High Street following the path of its Roman predecessor, up the long slope to the Westgate.

The imposing fourteenth-century Westgate and the more modest Kingsgate, which we will visit shortly, are the only survivors of the five gates which opened through the Roman, and then the mediaeval, walls to the long, straight roads stretching across the countryside. North, east, and south are still commemorated in the names of streets, but of the structures nothing now survives. Leland, in his *Itinerary* (1535-1543), mentions one small further gate: 'The 6th is by twixt north gate and est gate, no great thing but as a postern gate named Bourne Gate.'

The appearance of the High Street has suffered from a number of unsuitable intrusions, but nevertheless the diversity of styles still achieves a certain picturesqueness. The street has definite character, and the very fact that the company is so mixed lends a certain charm; the Pentice, the long colonnade which covers the southern pavement for the lower part of the street, greatly adds to the effect. One of the most venerable buildings in the street is Godbegot House, on the north side, which presents its mid-sixteenth-century front with jettied upper floors to the passer-by; while on the opposite side, where the colonnaded Pentice ends, stands the fifteenth-century Butter Cross, a graceful Gothic structure raised on an octagonal stepped platform, which received its name from the market at one time held round its base.

Behind the Cross, a passageway leads to the Cathedral and to the most attractive area of the City. The first sight of the Cathedral, one of the most important ecclesiastical buildings in Europe, with its long low outline almost hidden behind the trees of the Outer Close, is disappointing. It has none of the aspect of the Church Militant enjoyed by many cathedrals erected in dramatic or dominant positions. Here at Winchester, the vast, grey, stone structure seems to be sinking into the soft, green sward which surrounds it.

Perhaps the Normans would have chosen a bolder site for the great new cathedral they projected had not this been hallowed ground ever since the Old Minster had been raised here in the seventh century. It lay just to the north of the present Cathedral, and recent excavations have revealed its exact position and extent. It was in this building that Cnut, King of England, Norway and Denmark, was buried in 1035. It was just to the side of the crumbling Old Minster that Bishop Wakelin began in 1079 his magnificent new cathedral.

But it is not the work of the Norman builders which makes so intense an impact as one enters by the west door. The long avenue of clustered columns soaring to the fan vaulting, at a height which seems improbable from the exterior, is fourteenth-century work: between 1366 and 1404 William of Wykeham transformed the Cathedral by encasing the existing piers in Gothic shells and replacing the flat roof with the ribs and mouldings in the new manner. Only in the transepts does Wakelin's robust Norman work still survive, and to many these may seem the most beautiful parts of the

4 *Winchester Cathedral: looking into the nave from the north aisle*

whole structure.

The beauties and riches of this vast cathedral could fill a book of their own, and there is here no space to catalogue them all, but there are four objects of particular interest which, since they are not very assertive, I will mention. The first is the font which stands in the seventh bay on the north side of the nave. It dates from about 1150 and is made of Tournai marble, a material almost as hard and dark as bronze. The panels of the four sides are carved with scenes from the legend of St Nicholas, the patron saint of sailors, captives and children. There are three other similar fonts in Hampshire, at East Meon, St Mary Bourne, and St Michael's, Southampton, but the one at Winchester is the finest.

The three other objects are tombs, separated in date by several centuries, and by an eternity in spirit. The earliest is that of St Swithun, who died in 862. His bones are said to lie beneath the simple, tiled rectangle in the Retro Choir between the pompous fifteenth-century chantries of Cardinal Beaufort and William Waynflete. The position of this modest memorial is now emphasised by a form of wrought-iron baldachino set over it. The second is the sarcophagus of William Rufus in the middle of the chancel. The stone sides are not original, but the grey-green Purbeck marble top with its raised central panel and simple lines must date from the death of this much abused monarch in 1100. The third is the plain stone slab in the north aisle near the font commemorating the burial place of Jane Austen. The epitaph records her death on 18 July 1817 at the age of 41, and describes the nobility of her character and the 'extraordinary endowment of her mind', but makes no mention of her literary achievements.

The Close, which lies to the south of the Cathedral, is complex and broken in plan, partly owing to the fact that a number of the houses incorporate parts of the ancient Priory buildings. It has none of the ordered dignity of Salisbury, for example, but its charm, which is great, lies in the variety of the buildings which jostle round its grass swards and in the unexpected groups of attractive houses which open out of it.

The stone and flint gateway at the south-west corner leads into

5 *Winchester Cathedral: Bishop Fox's Chantry*

St Swithun Street, and so at right angles to the fifteenth-century Kingsgate, above which is the little church dedicated to this Hampshire saint. It was clearly this building that Anthony Trollope had in mind when describing in *The Warden* the church of St Cuthbert at Barchester:

> It is a singular little Gothic building, perched over a gateway, through which the Close is entered, and is approached by a flight of stone steps which lead down under the archway of the gate. It is no bigger than an ordinary room . . . but still it is a perfect church.

Running eastward outside the high wall of the Close is College Street, one of the prettiest streets in the City. Here in a little stucco-fronted house looking towards the Cathedral Jane Austen died. One thinks of her last words when her sister Cassandra asked her if she wished for anything. 'Only death,' she replied.

At the end of the street on the north side and backing on to the Close stands Wolvesey, the palace of the Bishops of Winchester, its dignified, grey walls rising amongst the trees of its garden. It is often said to have been designed by Sir Christopher Wren. There is no proof of this, although the great architect was at work on the abortive project for a palace for Charles II high on the west hill above the town at the time that Bishop Morley in 1684 was raising his episcopal palace in the meadows beside the Itchen. As originally built, it was of far greater extent than now, but about 1800 much of the palace was demolished—which accounts for its present rather truncated appearance—leaving only the west wing and the fifteenth-century chapel at its north end. Within the precincts of the Palace stand the ruins of Henry of Blois' twelfth-century castle, a building once of great extent as befitted the brother of King Stephen; it was probably stone from the castle, which was largely destroyed by the Cromwellians, that was used by Bishop Morley for the new palace. A charming walk leads from near the gate of Wolvesey past the ancient town walls and along the bank of the river to emerge just to the east of the Broadway.

As with the Cathedral, there is so much in the City which merits description that it is difficult to be properly selective. The street from which we have been enticed away leads very naturally to the College, the gateway to which stands nearly opposite Wolvesey. Founded by William of Wykeham in 1387, it forms, with its courts, cloisters, playing fields and buildings varying in date from the fourteenth to the twentieth century, one of the most attractive groups of school buildings in the country.

But we have lingered too long in the valley and we should now mount the long western slope to the Castle, which stands a little above and to the south of the Westgate, and formed as it were an annex to the original rectangular plan of the City. Only the Great Hall survives of the royal building in which Henry III and Prince Arthur, son of Henry VII, were born, in which Henry VIII entertained the Emperor Charles V, and where the ceremonies following the marriage of Mary with Philip of Spain were held. Basically it dates from the thirteenth century, and the tall, clustered columns supporting Gothic arches are of this period, but drastic restoration in 1874 has laid a heavy hand on the stonework. For many years the assize court, erected like a stage scene within these ancient walls, has blocked a view of the Hall, and will do so until the new courts are completed.

At the west end of the Hall, disconsolately facing the back of the temporary court, is the splendid bronze statue of Queen Victoria, the work of that remarkable sculptor Alfred Gilbert, one of the finest exponents of the *Art Nouveau* style. On the wall above the Queen's head hangs the great circular board, 17 feet across, known as King Arthur's Round Table. Should anyone doubt the truth of the Arthurian legends, here is evidence of their authenticity; and let no one be deflected by the fact that it seems unlikely that the table is more than seven centuries old.

There is one further group of buildings that it is essential to visit before leaving Winchester for the countryside, and this is the Hospital of St Cross. The road from the Kingsgate originally led due southward past the College and through the water meadows bordering the Itchen to the gate of the Hospital. To some degree this is still the case, but development which has joined St Cross to Winchester and the reduction of the southern stretch of the road to a 'No Thoroughfare' has obscured this fact, and the principal entrance to the Hospital is from the Roman road to Bittern.

St Cross is a group of great picturesqueness: perhaps no almshouses in the country have a setting of more beauty. From the entrance court a gateway under the Beaufort Tower leads into the great Quadrangle and there on the far side rises the massive form of the Norman church, the greater part of which dates from the second half of the twelfth century and is the successor to the church built by the founder, Henry de Blois, in 1136. The chancel and transepts are particularly rich examples of the Norman style, in spite of a rather overenthusiastic restoration under the auspices of Butterfield in the nineteenth century; but when it is realised the condition of decay to which this splendid building had been reduced, one feels grateful to the Victorians for saving it from complete collapse. Here is the description of its condition from Robert Mudie's *Hampshire* of 1839:

> As a place of worship this church has nothing to recommend it. The part divided off for this purpose is small; the pews and the screens, or rather partitions, are tasteless; there is no organ; and the apparatus for ringing the bells, which is very conspicuous, puts one in mind of the machinery of a theatre. This portion consists of the choir and part of the transepts; the nave, the aisles, and the remainder of these being open and free to the winds.

When we criticise, as we often do, the drastic restorations of ecclesiastical buildings carried out by the Victorians, we are apt to forget the appalling neglect with which several previous generations had treated these structures, often of the highest merit. Miss Mitford's description in *Our Village* (1842) of the condition of Bramley church in the north part of the County could no doubt have been applied to many parish churches of less importance than Bramley. Here are her words: 'The church is small, simple, decaying, almost ruinous.' My eulogies of the church as it is now will be found in Chapter Four.

Along the west side of the St Cross Quadrangle is the long, low range of Brethren's dwellings, which with the Great Hall and Kitchens on the north side were built by Cardinal Beaufort about 1445, while the east side is closed by a narrow Ambulatory constructed in an engaging mixture of bricks and stone. Beyond the river and the meadows in the shallow valley where the Hospital stands rises the rotund form of St Catherine's Hill, crowned by its group of beech trees, a natural feature which dominates the view both from the College and the Hospital. It is impossible to conceive of a place more conducive to a peaceful old age and to a tranquil resignation to the adversity of Noble Poverty.

Since this chapter covers Winchester and the countryside round it it may be a convenient start to follow the course of the river Itchen from the boundary of the City to its source away to the east—a total distance, including its meanderings, of less than 15 miles. It is a river of charm rather than of size, and one may add that it is remarkably well-behaved, for even in the wettest season the clear chalk water seldom floods out over the meadows which border its course.

From Winchester the river valley runs almost due north, accompanied for some of this length by the Winchester by-pass. After less than a couple of miles in this direction it turns east, and finally southward to its source, which is no more than eight miles in a direct line from Winchester. The names of the villages along the first stretch of the river are curiously repetitive. First come the four Worthys—Headbourne, Kings, Abbots and Martyr. None of these villages which are scattered along the valley road to Alresford are of particular interest except the first, where the little parish church dedicated to St Swithun is outstanding.

Although close to the highway, it lies so low in a depression that it is easy to pass this inconspicuous building—one of the earliest churches in the county—without noticing it. The greater part of the nave and part of the chancel is pre-Conquest, with long-and-short Saxon work, while the sturdy tower topped by a wooden belfry is thirteenth century. The style is typical of many in the county, where tall towers are a rarity and spires, except in nineteenth-century buildings, almost unknown. The remarkable feature, which gives this little church importance, is the rood carved in stone on what was originally the outer face of the west wall above a doorway. In the fifteenth century it was covered by a building consisting of a chamber below and a small chapel above. The floor has now been removed and the whole serves as a vestry.

The rood has been sadly defaced, and the figures, which were in low relief, have been cut almost level with the wall. This mutilation is attributed to Bishop Horne of Winchester (1560-1580), who ordered all crucifixes in his diocese to be destroyed. But it can still be seen that it represents Christ, flanked by Our Lady and St John, and above the head of the central figure the hand of the Almighty appears out of a cloud. Even in its mutilated form it is a rare Saxon survival.

But the name Headbourne Worthy may have a familiar sound to a section of the community quite different to that which is interested in Saxon roods, in fact to the gardening community, for it is here on the chalk slope above the church that Mr Lewis Palmer raised a number of lime-tolerant plants and of these the hardy *Agapanthus*, the Headbourne Worthy hybrid, is perhaps the best-known and has brought distinction to innumerable gardens.

The other three Worthys call for little mention. They contain a few picturesque thatched cottages, and Worthy Park in Abbots Worthy is a handsome yellow brick house designed by Sir Robert Smirke, the architect of the British Museum, about 1825, and now converted to office use; but otherwise they are architecturally rather disordered little villages.

Beyond the last of the Worthys a road turns southward and crosses the two branches of the Itchen, which flow through this wide shallow valley, to the village of Easton on the gentle rise above the river. There are some attractive houses here, but it is the church which, both in interest and in size, is well above the average for Hampshire. It dates almost entirely from about 1200, although it did not escape mid-nineteenth-century 'improvements', which included apparently the rather eccentric shingled summit to the tower. The site is charming, with the churchyard sloping down towards the river and the leafy meadows which border it.

Instead of returning to the highway on the north side of the valley, it is highly rewarding to take the little lane from Easton which runs along the south side to the next group of villages with almost similar names—Avington, Ovington, and Lovington. The lane soon leaves the meadows and crosses a cattle grid into Avington Park, and the rose-pink façade of the house comes into view lying low beyond a wide sheet of water. A wonderfully English scene this, admirably composed with all the skill of the eighteenth century, so that trees, water and pastures form a perfect setting for the house. The architecture is principally of the early eighteenth century and is not perhaps of great distinction except for the majestic portico in wood which fills the recessed centre of the building. The house is open at certain times, but except for the handsome ballroom on the first floor the interior is not of great interest.

On no account should Avington church be missed: it is an eighteenth-century gem. It lies south of the house close to the small road which passes through the village. It is in brick and was built during the three years following 1768, and by happy chance has retained the full flavour of the period—box pews, pulpit, font, a fine marble monument to the Marchioness of Carnarvon, and, anyhow until lately, the velvet-bound prayer books in the squire's pews. For a number of years the estate belonged to the Shelley-Rolls family, a strange conjunction of the poetical and the mechanical, and indeed Sir John was a collateral descendant of the poet and his wife the sister of the creator of the most famous make of motor cars in the world.

On the same side of the valley lies the village of Ovington, which has a prosperous air, for many of the cottages have been adapted to the use of the gentry, attracted perhaps to this quiet village by the excellent, and highly expensive, fishing in this broad and shallow stretch of the Itchen. The village has the distinction of having given its name to a square and a street in South Kensington, the two properties—urban and country—in the early nineteenth century having been in the possession of the same owner.

Across the valley on the northern slope are the villages of Itchen Abbas and Itchen Stoke, both lying on either side of the Winchester to Alresford highway which becomes dangerously constricted as it passes amongst the cottages of the latter. In both villages the churches are nineteenth-century, that in Itchen Stoke being a free rendering of the Sainte Chapelle, its tall form making a somewhat startling feature of the Hampshire countryside.

East of Itchen Stoke is the junction of the river Alre, coming in from the north, with the Itchen, but pursuing our plan to follow the latter river to its source, we take a small road which accompanies the much reduced stream through the meadows to Tichborne. The place is no more than a hamlet with a few cottages, a pub, a former rectory—all thatched—strung along the lane. In a commanding position to the south of the cottages stands the church, which I find one of the most engaging of the smaller parish churches in the county, partly perhaps because it escaped drastic nineteenth-century restoration. Here little alteration has been made since 1703, when the tower, in rosy brick with blue headers, was added at the west end to the ancient structure, which is pre-Conquest with late twelfth-century aisles. The interior has great charm, with two simple, sturdy arches cut through the thick Saxon walls on either side to form north and south aisles. It was the work, one must suppose, of local stonemasons who enlarged the chancel arch at the same time and scorned all decoration or embellishment. The nave still contains its high Jacobean pews.

The north aisle forms the Tichborne chapel and is still dedicated to Catholic worship. It contains a number of fine monuments to the family, of which that to Sir Benjamin Tichborne, who died in 1621, and his wife is the most magnificent. The two life-sized figures are recumbent on the tomb with their children, on a smaller scale, portrayed on the panel below them.

Tichborne Park lies low by the river which has given its name to the place and to the family. which is probably the oldest in the county. The name always recalls the famous trial of 1873, which lasted for almost a year, when Arthur Orton, the butcher from Wapping, claimed to be the vanished Roger Tichborne. But was he Orton? Although he lost his claim and was sent to jail, there were many strange and unresolved features of the case.

Through the damp meadows, brilliant in summer with the white

6 Wren's building at Winchester College

tufts of *spirea* and the golden flowers of irises and kingcups, the course of the stream—for it is no longer a river—comes to Cheriton, where it divides and passes in two branches through the village and provides a most agreeable feature of a place of modest architectural distinction, but of agreeable layout round a spacious green. It seems strange that William Cobbett in 1882 saw it as 'a little, hard, iron village, where all seems as old as the hills that surround it'. It certainly has now changed for the better.

To students of the Civil War this village will be familiar for the battle to which it gave its name—a battle crucial to the fortunes of the Royalists. It took place amongst the undulations to the east of Cheriton, where the high pastures must have been as empty of habitation as they are today. In March 1644 it became clear that an engagement was imminent between the Cavaliers under Lord Hopton, quartered in the Winchester area, and the Roundheads, who Sir William Waller was leading through Surrey into Hampshire. By the 28th of the month the two armies, each consisting of about 10,000 men, were poised for the engagement which became known as the battle of Cheriton. The Cavaliers were massed on the high ground south of Alresford, and the Roundheads were on the long ridge north of Hinton Ampner. About ten in the morning the battle began amongst the hedges and coppices on the undulations between the two armies, and before nightfall the Cavaliers had been defeated with such losses that the lanes are said 'to have run with blood'. It was a defeat from which the King's cause never recovered.

We have now almost reached the source of the Itchen, which is barely a mile to the south in the neighbouring parish of Kilmeston. The river rises in a little willow-filled dell by the side of the narrow road from Cheriton to Kilmeston. It must be owned that in most summers it hardly deserves the name 'river', for it is generally dry, but in wet seasons the clear stream flows strongly, and picking up the water of other springs in the adjacent meadows soon develops into a considerable brook.

On the hill above the source stand the house, church, and hamlet of Hinton Ampner which natural patriotism compels me to mention —although it barely qualifies for inclusion in a book as selective

7 *Winchester College: the Cloister*

as this—since it is there that I was born and still live so that for much of my life I have looked out over this undulating countryside of arable fields and woodlands which in its unpretentious way has—at least for me—immeasurable charm. Even Cobbett acknowledged that it was 'a pretty country' in spite of the sad decay of farming and country life which he observed all about this area. But I have enlarged on Hinton Ampner elsewhere [*Hinton Ampner: A Hampshire Manor*, Batsford, 1968], and will say no more of it here.

On the north side of the long ridge of high ground which ends at the source of the Itchen lies the village of Bramdean astride the Winchester to Petersfield highway. The name has the pleasant Saxon meaning of 'the valley where the broom grows', and no doubt woods covered the gentle slopes on either hand. Now the charm of the village lies in the number of eighteenth- and early nineteenth-century houses which it contains, and the attractive public house, the Fox, with its wide, wooden, bow window, which may date from an even earlier period.

It is time, however, to turn northward and follow the river Alre from its junction with the Itchen to the main town of this immediate area, Alresford. It is a place which has expanded greatly in the past few decades and much building has taken place on the south and west sides, but in spite of the increase of population the centre retains its character to a remarkable degree. There are three main streets: West Street and East Street along which the Winchester to Alton highway takes its straight course through the town; and Broad Street, which branches northward at the junction of the two other streets. Both the first and last are of generous width, and are lined with houses and shops mostly with eighteenth-century fronts, but which in some cases are modest classical dresses covering bodies of greater age. There is little architecture of great distinction, but the variety of bricks and stucco, and the determined individuality of almost every little building, give these streets charm and interest. The church standing on the top of the rise a little to the south of the junction of the three streets is well-placed, but is not of great interest.

It was in a house on the west side of Broad Street that Mary Russell

Mitford, the novelist, was born in 1787, and she may well have had the little town of her birth in mind when she wrote her village stories—although they were principally founded on her home at Three Mile Cross which is a few miles beyond the boundaries of the county. The family left Alresford when Mary was only ten years old, the new house at Three Mile Cross being built by her father from part of £20,000 which he was fortunate enough to win in a lottery. It represented a brief moment of affluence which Mr Mitford soon extinguished by his uncontrollable extravagance.

The proper designation of the town is New Alresford, but now the adjective is only used to differentiate it from the village of Old Alresford, for as a town there is nothing 'new' about it. There were already some dwellings here when Bishop de Lucy rebuilt it on a large scale in the twelfth century, and it soon flourished exceedingly so that two centuries later it was considered one of the ten great wool markets in the country. But thereafter the industry declined and a devastating fire, a calamity to which the town seems to have been particularly prone during its history, reduced it to a place of poverty. Revival was again hindered when the Royalists set fire to it after the Battle of Cheriton, but an even more disastrous fire occurred in 1689, when the greater part of the town was destroyed. Thus only a few of the houses which appear from behind the eighteenth-century façades can be older than this date.

Old Alresford, the senior partner in name, is much the junior in size, and is in fact no more than a scattered village. From the bottom of Broad Street a road runs along the top of the vast embankment raised by the active Bishop Lucy in order to form a great lake with the waters from the many springs which rise in the valley to the east and by this means to feed a canal to join Alresford to Winchester, and so by the river Itchen to Southampton. As the sixteenth-century Leland described it:

> This river [the Alre] first beginnith with a great number of fair sylver springs a good mile above Alresford: and these resorting to a botom make a good brode lak, communely caullied Alsford Pond.

He makes no mention of the Bishop's embankment to which this congregation of water was due, and I must confess that the mechanics of this enterprise have never been clear to me, but apparently they worked, though this artificial waterway no longer functions. However, as one drives along the embankment there still is the lake on the right, but now much reduced from the 200 acres of its original size, and on the left, at a much lower level, is a large expanse of watercress beds—a great industry of this area.

On a rise beyond the embankment stands the church, its sturdy, mid-eighteenth-century, brick tower so placed, that it can be seen across the valley from a mile or two away as one approaches Alresford along the Winchester road. This tower and a magnificent marble monument in the interior to the first wife of Admiral Lord Rodney, who died in 1757, are the principal features of the church. The Admiral owned and largely rebuilt the adjacent house.

To the north of the church is a large brick house once the rectory, a reminder of the days when to be the Rector of Old Alresford was to enjoy a singularly lucrative cure of souls. In the early nineteenth century it was held by the seventh Earl of Guilford in conjunction with the Mastership of St Cross. By intensive depredations on the endowments of the latter he was able to enlarge the Rectory house and live in splendour at Old Alresford, though his way of life was eventually somewhat curtailed by a judicial investigation in 1853. However, the money he appropriated was not ill-spent and this very agreeable place now fulfils a useful function as the Winchester Diocese House.

North-east of the Alresfords the country rises to a wide area of uplands technically known as the Hampshire Downs. These are not downs in the true sense, but high, open, arable country with a number of villages amidst the undulations. They rise in places to a height of over 700 feet, and extend in a wide sweep between Alresford and Basingstoke. The rather austere landscape in this area particularly appealed to Cobbett, who clearly found it more sympathetic than the leafy meadows bordering the Itchen. In *Rural Rides* he wrote:

> These high down-countries are not garden plats, like Kent, but they have . . . always been my delight. Large sweeping downs, and deep dells here and there, with villages amongst lofty trees, are my great delight.

This description could pass for the greater part of the chalky heart of the county, the central area of which this chapter covers. In the pockets of deep soil, of which there are many, oak woods grow well; while on many of the dry hills former generations of landowners have planted groves of beech trees which, although growing slowly to maturity on the thin soil, give beauty and variety to these uplands.

The diversity in the nature of the soil, sometimes chalk, sometimes clay, but almost everywhere with a strong limey content, favours a wide range of indigenous shrubs, such as maple, may, sloe, hazel, buckthorn, wayfaring tree, spindle, elder, holly, crab-apple; while about the countryside, where not within reach of cattle, the dark masses of yew trees can be seen in the hedgerows, and on some of the downs junipers and daphnes flourish.

A mile or two to the north of Old Alresford, where woods cover the lower slopes of the uplands, stands a curious little building by the side of a lane to a farm house: Godsfield Chapel. It dates from the late fourteenth century, and consists of a small chapel with a priest's house at one end, forming together a single rectangle with a projection containing a staircase on the north side. Its interest is perhaps principally to the antiquary.

Of the villages in this high country Bentworth is the most attractive containing for a smallish village a surprising number of 'gentry' houses, and also a handsome church dating largely from the thirteenth century. The stout, circular piers of the nave with carved capitals are excellent survivals of the period. A little over a mile to the north is Lasham, noteworthy not for its architecture but as a centre of gliding. Here, in suitable weather, the machines, like great silent birds, float apparently effortlessly above a former wartime airfield.

Bearing west from Old Alresford away from these uplands, the road to Basingstoke crosses Abbotstone Down from which there is a fine view across the wide valleys of the Itchen and the Alre to the long ridge of the Milbarrow hills upwards of ten miles away to the south.

To the south of the down there once stood the great house of Abbotstone, the property of the Duke of Bolton. It was described in 1719 by Pavey as 'a large noble brick house edged with stone . . . built after the Italian manner opening a vista from one end of the house to the other . . . there are above 100 rooms in the house'. Of this magnificence there now remains no visible sign, except a stretch of wall perhaps once surrounding a kitchen garden. The house seems, indeed, to have been demolished almost before it was completed.

Another great house, barely a mile from Abbotstone, is also doomed to destruction, and may in fact have disappeared before these words reach print. This is The Grange, the vast mansion created by the Drummond family from the designs of William Wilkins in 1809. The Grecian shell, however, covered a seventeenth-century body designed by William Samwell, while the two Cockerells, father and son, made further additions in the nineteenth century. The heyday of The Grange was after the purchase of the estate by Alexander Baring, later Lord Ashburton, in 1817.

It was here that Harriet, Lady Ashburton entertained Thomas and Jane Carlyle at her brilliant and intellectual houseparties. The Carlyles' first visit was in 1844, and, although Thomas enjoyed his entry into high society, Jane disliked these social activities to such a degree that a rift was almost caused in their affection. In her Journal in 1855 she wrote: 'If we had been left in the sphere of life we belong to, how much better it would have been for us in many ways.' However, relief was at hand, for in 1857 Lady Ashburton died, and in the following year Lord Ashburton married Louisa Stewart MacKenzie, who was perfectly sympathetic to both Carlyles, and the rift in the Chelsea *ménage* was healed.

North of the park of The Grange the road to Basingstoke passes through the three Candover villages, Brown, Chilton and Preston. Of these the last is much the largest, and contains several handsome eighteenth-century houses, which can be faintly glimpsed from the highway, but Chilton is the most interesting on account of its underground church. It is in fact the Norman crypt of a demolished structure, which was brought to light by an enterprising incumbent about 40 years ago. It is stoutly built of flint with a round-headed chancel arch in stone opening to an apse. Another feature of this little village worth observing is the broad avenue of yew trees about half a mile in length—an avenue much admired by Cobbett—which runs up the long slope to the lane from the Alresford road to Preston Candover.

From these three villages, all lying in the valley of the Candover Brook which joins the Itchen near Alresford, the road mounts the long ridge of hills which forms the boundary between the great chalk heart of the county and the low-lying area of clay country in the north-east. From the summit of the hill before the road descends into the plain there is a view away to distant hills beyond the Thames valley and it is an occasion when distance definitely lends enchantment for the country over which the eye wanders is not in fact a picturesque area.

We will, however, leave the plain for Chapter Four, and turn westwards and pass down from the high ground and across the Roman road which is the highway from Winchester to Basingstoke to the scattered little village of Micheldever, where the church of St Mary will fascinate those who care for the eccentric in ecclesiastical architecture. The tall west tower in flint and stone, standing nobly on rising ground, dates from the first half of the sixteenth century, and this is adjoined by one bay of the original thirteenth-century nave. The remainder was destroyed by fire in 1806, and in its place a spacious octagon was erected by George Dance in brick which is singularly Gothic in style. Perhaps to remedy this profane spirit a timid Gothic chancel was added in 1881. The whole composition, if indeed a building so unhomogeneous can be called such, is at least unusual; but a more soothing note is supplied by three monuments, designed by Flaxman, to members of the Baring family.

This branch of the family lived at Stratton, the fine park of which is bounded by the Roman road. This place was the home of Rachel, Lady Russell, whose husband was executed on a flimsy pretext by Charles II, and many of her heartbroken letters were addressed from

Stratton. Her house gave place in the eighteenth century to one designed by George Dance; this in its turn has been replaced by a house in contemporary style.

Less than a couple of miles to the west of Micheldever is a church of very different character—Stoke Charity. The church stands in a meadow with a few houses scattered round at a little distance, but the manor house which once adjoined it has disappeared. The exterior is not dramatic, but the massive, early Norman arcade on the north side of the aisle is highly impressive in so small a building, while the Mass of St Gregory carved in stone is a rare fifteenth-century survival. There are also a number of handsome monuments from the fifteenth to the seventeenth centuries, which agreeably crowd the church. Altogether it is perhaps one of the more interesting small churches in the county.

Stoke Charity lies due north of Winchester, and continuing our anti-clockwise tour round the City, there is little to catch the eye as one turns south-west except the charm of the pastoral and sequestered countryside. Across this area runs another of the Roman roads, that to Cirencester. Passing through Littleton with its racing stud one comes to Sparsholt, where the attractive, late seventeenth-century brick front of Lainston House shows well from the road. The house stands on a rise facing down a long, loosely planted avenue which stretches away to the Winchester road. On the west side of the house, but invisible from the highway, stand the ruins of the Norman chapel in which Elizabeth Chudleigh, who later became notorious as the 'bigamous Duchess', was married in 1744 to her first husband Augustus Hervey. Twenty-five years later she went through a form of marriage with the Duke of Kingston. Three years after the Duke's death in 1773 she was tried for bigamy before the House of Lords and found guilty but, as a peeress, escaped sentence.

South of Sparsholt is an area of high, undulating chalk country, well-wooded and sparsely populated as is usual where the soil is thin and poor. Across this area, running almost due west, is still another of the spoke-like complex of Roman roads emerging from Winchester. This is the road to Old Sarum, now for much of its length no more than a track passing across Pitt and Farley Downs.

8 The Beaufort Tower, Hospital of St Cross, Winchester

On the highest point of the latter stands an obelisk erected in the middle of the eighteenth century by Sir Paulet St John commemorating the feat of a favourite hunter which jumped into a chalkpit and landed 25 feet below without injury to itself or its rider. It was not a feat, one must suppose, to be encouraged or repeated.

From the down there is a tremendous view seemingly over half Hampshire and away to the hills above Salisbury. For many centuries the St John family owned Farley, their house (now vanished) having presumably been close to the church, appropriately dedicated to St John, which stands in the fields remote from any village. It is basically a simple twelfth-century structure with eighteenth-century alterations, but the principal features are the monuments to the members of the St John family. There is a fine altar tomb to William St John in ruff and hose, who died in 1609, and a moving memorial to John St John, who died in 1627 at the age of 24, and to his widow and infant son, who followed him to the grave within a few months.

A mile or two to the east of Farley are the ruins of Merdon Castle, rising within a fine, circular earthwork. Barely sufficient stonework now survives to show the style and extent of the building which Bishop Henry de Blois erected in 1138, but it is known to have been a place of grandeur and importance, and less a fortified castle than a palace. However, in the fourteenth century it was abandoned and now, after six centuries of decay, little survives but a few lengths of wall seven feet thick.

The Castle stands on the northern edge of the Park of Hursley, a mid-Georgian house vastly aggrandised in the early years of this century. It now serves as offices and laboratories for the company of IBM. In an earlier house lived for many years Richard Cromwell, the ineffectual son of Oliver, the Lord Protector. In 1649 he married Dorothy Major, the heiress of Hursley. She was the daughter of Richard Major, who was said to be an unscrupulous oppressor of his tenantry, especially after the execution of King Charles when Oliver was in control of the country. Richard lived quietly at Hursley until the death of his father in 1658 brought him into sudden and unwelcome prominence. His Protectorate of seven months and 28 days passes almost unnoticed in history, and at its termination the un-

9 *The Itchen at Ovington, near Alresford*

fortunate Richard left England for 20 years of exile. In 1680, however, he was permitted to return—a magnanimous gesture on the part of Charles II—and under the name of Clarke lived into the reign of Queen Anne, at least part of the time at Hursley, where he was buried in 1712.

The church, which stands at the west end of the attractive village, was rebuilt in a rather dull fourteenth-century style at the expense of John Keble, the rector from 1836 until his death 30 years later. It has interest as the creation of the leader of the Oxford Movement, while the stained glass was made by William Wailes under the supervision of Butterfield, whose hand can be seen in other details of the interior. Perhaps reluctantly, Keble allowed the fine monument to Richard Cromwell's daughter Elizabeth, who died in 1731, to survive. It is designed by the rather obscure architect George Sampson.

Keble held the living of Hursley in conjunction with Otterbourne, a fairly large village lying astride the road from Winchester to Southampton—a village to which comparative peace has come by the building of the new by-pass to Chandler's Ford. In a house on the east side of the road Charlotte Yonge, the novelist, was born in 1823, and here she lived for the greater part of her very productive literary life. She became a close friend of Keble and an ardent supporter of the Oxford Movement. She devoted all profits from her novels, of which *The Heir of Redcliffe* and *The Daisy Chain* were the most successful, to various religious objects. She died in 1901, and a simple granite moulding surrounds her grave, which is at the foot of the cross erected in memory of John Keble.

The church was designed and erected by Charlotte's father William with the aid of Owen Carter in 1837, and although the blue-grey brick in which it is built is melancholy in colour as a structure it is not unsuccessful. The additions made in 1875 are less attractive.

Behind the church lies the large park of Cranbury, through the border of which the new road passes. The house was largely rebuilt in the late eighteenth century by Sir Nathaniel Dance-Holland, the brother of the architect George Dance, and the design may well be the result of a successful fraternal combination. There are several fine rooms; the ballroom is particularly splendid. The house is not open to the public.

Almost opposite the church a small road runs eastward across the wide valley of the Itchen. The river has here become of considerable size and flows swiftly through the deep, quiet meadows in a number of streams, so that the road passes over a series of narrow bridges until it reaches Brambridge. The house, rebuilt after a fire in 1872, is gaunt and grim, but on the east side there is a splendid double avenue of lime trees stretching across the flat park to the Twyford road. The property was inherited in the second half of the eighteenth century by Walter Smythe, the father of Mrs FitzHerbert, and he may well have been the planter of the avenue. Maria spent much of her youth here before her brief marriage in 1775 to Edward Weld, who died within a year. Soon after she married Thomas FitzHerbert but was left a widow a second time in 1781, and four years later her clandestine marriage to the Prince of Wales took place.

The distance as the crow flies from this lower valley of the Itchen, before it passes into the urban area of Eastleigh and Southampton, to its source is little more than eight miles; but the crow in taking a straight line has to surmount the long ridge of down-like hills which stretches almost from Winchester to the Meon Valley. There is, however, one point at which the crow should break his flight, and this is to inspect the little church at Chilcombe. For those on *terra firma* the hamlet can be reached either from the Winchester by-pass (A 33) or from the A 272—it lies in an angle between the two. The church is not easy to find, for it stands south of the sparse collection of houses where the narrow lane degenerates into a track running up through a wood on to the downs. It is a simple little building, reminiscent of Boarhunt, which we shall visit in Chapter Six, both in date and position on a steep north slope. It was begun apparently in 1060 and has suffered little alteration. It is built of flint and stone, and has a weather-boarded bell turret at the west end; the original south doorway is still in use, but that on the north side has been walled up. As in all little churches of this early pre-Conquest date, the chancel arch is extremely narrow, and in the floor of the chancel is a panel of early English tiles. How fortunate, one feels, were these obscure churches with no rich patron or parishioners to effect drastic, if well-intentioned, restorations during the nineteenth century.

From this interlude we can return to the roads which pass along this high ground to the east of Winchester. There are two: first the highway from Winchester to Petersfield, and then the road to Warnford which branches off it. From various points on both of these there are superb views both to north and south. As one looks out over these undulating, misty landscapes, one realises why the art of water-colour painting is a field in which the English are pre-eminent. Here before one, in soft and varied tones and beneath a gently clouded sky, woodlands and fields stretch away to a distant blue horizon.

The most beautiful of these views is from Cheesefoot Head on the Petersfield road. The elevation is not very great—just under 600 feet—but from this point there is an uninterrupted view both northward and southward over a huge area of the county. To the north the eye is carried over the inexplicable basin of the Devil's Punch Bowl, away over the valley of the Itchen to the mass of high downs which fills the north-western corner of the county 20 miles away.

Southward the prospect is even more beautiful and more distant. The high ground falls away, gentle fold on gentle fold, in what appears to be a long, indented valley, with wooded hills far apart on either hand. On a clear day this seeming valley is terminated by a silver streak of water which is the Solent, while beyond the water rise the dim but majestic outlines of the downs of St Boniface and St Catherine, marking the southern extremity of the Isle of Wight 30 miles distant.

CHAPTER TWO

The New Forest and the southern seaboard

Several of the chapters in this book cover ill-shapen areas, areas whose confines have been dictated by rivers or hills, or more often by those changes in the soil which have so profound an effect on landscape, population and architecture. This chapter, however, covers a neatly compact area which is roughly a rectangle bounded by Southampton Water on the east side, the Solent and Christchurch Bay on the south, and the county boundary on the west, while to the north, a line follows the junction of Hampshire with Wiltshire south of Salisbury and passes the northern fringe of the New Forest to reach the lower waters of the Test. The only serious excrescence to these tidy frontiers is that strange protruberance of the county to the west, which is known as the Martin peninsula.

Although compact in form, the area is diverse in character, for there is much industrial development on the east side along Southampton Water, and a wide belt of building, mostly of a domestic sort, in the south-west area where Bournemouth and Christchurch are in a constant condition of expansion. Away from these busy districts lie the many square miles of the Forest, stretching away from near the coast to the imaginary line we have drawn across the county south of Romsey about 14 miles away in a direct line to the north. Naturally, then, the area covered by this chapter is one where the beauties of nature predominate over those of architecture, for the towns in the forest country, with the exception of Beaulieu, are not of outstanding interest, while the villages are mostly agreeable collections of thatched cottages which settle pleasantly into their leafy setting.

However, in a perambulation round the borders of the Forest, on which I propose to lead you, it will be found that there are a number of places and buildings which are far from insignificant, and indeed can compete in importance with anything in the county. But in the background of these works of man always lie the great expanses of the Forest itself, which in spite of various assaults on its integrity, such as the unavoidable enclosures made by the Forestry Commission for the regeneration of the woodlands, maintains its wild and Arcadian beauty to a very high degree. One can still wander among the glades and groves and by little brackish streams in the valleys, or on the wind-blown areas of open heath, with a prospect of rolling country, aubergine or purple according to the season, extending fold beyond fold as far as the eye can reach, and experience a feeling of assimilation into primaeval nature. There are wide areas where the poor, sour soil will support nothing but heather and gorse with a few indifferent Scots pine, and these barren areas give way to deep, wooded valleys where on the kinder soil green glades stretch away between the massive trunks of oaks and the silver boles of beech trees, with an undergrowth of hawthorn and the rich glossy leaves of holly, in a wild and mysterious beauty which the art of man could never emulate.

All about the Forest, often grazing unconcernedly close to the busy highway or in the villages, can be seen the ponies. They are the descendants of the small wild horses which are known to have been here at the time of the Normans, and they may well have ancestry far longer than that. There are now about 2,500 ponies, most of which are mares, for the stallions are limited to a little more than 100. They have a definite family life of their own, keeping to their own small groups, and restricting their movements to one area of the Forest. The feed is poor, and during the depth of the winter the ponies must graze all day to keep alive. There are, however, areas of better grass where the land was ploughed during the last war and has since been reseeded, and these welcome spaces are well patronised by the ponies. The deer, mostly fallow deer, are the other natural denizens of the Forest. They are less popular with the inhabitants than the ponies for, although shy, they emerge from woodland at night and do infinite damage to gardens, crops and young plantations.

The New Forest survives as a true forest, wild and romantic, in spite of the highways which stretch across it. It is quite unlike other forests of Hampshire such as the Forest of Bere, which is now rather a district than a forest and in parts a highly populated one, or Alice Holt Forest, which has been thoroughly tamed in the interests of sylviculture. The New Forest remains much as it has been for 1,000 years, or indeed for ever. No guidance is needed for those who wish to explore its beauties: everyone will find those parts which please him best, whether it is the open spaces or the thickly wooded, the wilder or the more domesticated areas. But if no guide is needed, perhaps a little about the history of the Forest will not be out of place.

The tradition which persisted for centuries, that William the Conqueror ruthlessly depopulated the area of the New Forest in order to improve the hunting, in the process destroying villages, parish churches and peasants' cottages, is now exploded. The originator of this highly coloured version of the true facts, appears to have been Henry of Huntingdon who, writing about 1135, expressed himself as follows:

> Beasts of the chase he [William] cherished as if they were his children; so that to form the hunting-ground of the New Forest he caused churches and villages to be destroyed, and, driving out the people, made it a habitation for deer.

This was too good a story not to be repeated by future chroniclers, and thus it passed into history. It was conveniently forgotten that the area had been the hunting ground of the Saxon Kings long before the Normans landed on these shores, and further that so much of the soil was so miserably poor and sour that it could never have supported the most industrious peasant.

However it is certainly true that William formed what was called the New Forest in 1079 and drew up regulations prohibiting hunting and the killing of deer by any except those to whom he gave special permission. These rules were principally designed to control the activities of the Saxon landowners who remained a menace to the Norman régime. The real villain was William Rufus, who undoubtedly oppressed the scanty population of the Forest, and enforced the penalty of death for any infringement of the regulations. It was singularly appropriate that Walter Tyrell's arrow should have killed him in the Forest where he had caused much misery. The site of this fortunate occurrence is marked by a stone in a woodland known as Canterton Glen just north of the A 31 between Cadnam and Stoney Cross.

Before long it became clear that this royal domain, which had been preserved solely for pleasure, was of inestimable national value as a reservoir of timber for the navy. Beech trees thrived on the chalk and oak trees grew well on the areas of clay soil, and these could be conveniently brought to the dockyards to Portsmouth and the neighbourhood by sea. William Gilpin, writing his *Forest Scenery* in 1791, observed that the oak trees 'seldom rise into lofty stems, as oaks usually do in richer soils: but their branches . . . are more adapted to what shipbuilders call *knees* and *elbows*'. This formation, so useful in the construction of ships, has no doubt been a characteristic of the oaks of the New Forest throughout its history.

At first it must have seemed that the reservoir of timber for shipbuilding was inexhaustible, but as the ships of the navy increased in number it became clear that the royal forests were gradually running out of suitable trees. Under the Tudors various regulations were drawn up designed to encourage the growth of young trees, but not until the reign of James I was a constructive plan made for enclosing areas in which saplings would be protected from deer and grazing cattle. The areas within the fences were to be ploughed and to be planted with acorns 'by men's hands'. These instructions applied to all the royal forests, and by this means it was hoped to increase the areas of productive woodlands by as much as 3,400 acres a year.

In 1609 John Norden was sent into the Forest to make a comprehensive survey of all the coppices in the area, and the plans and report he made are still preserved in the Record Office. The coppices which he charted were those that had been fenced for regeneration in mediaeval and Tudor times, and he marked on his map the three different methods of protecting the young trees from deer and other

10 *Micheldever church*

11 *St Catherine's Hill*

12 *The Itchen near Winchester*

animals. Some were surrounded by a fence on a bank with an outside ditch, some by the fence alone, and some by a hedge. The two last defences have long since disappeared, but the banks and ditches surrounding irregular-shaped areas of woodland still survive in some cases.

Anyone interested in mediaeval forestry—this is perhaps rather a specialised hobby—can see an admirable example in the woodlands known as North and South Bentley which lie to the north of the A 31 near Stoney Cross. Beyond the desolate area known as Ocknell Plain, which is still criss-crossed by the mouldering runways and roads of wartime occupation and whose soil is so impervious that water stands in pools for days after rain has fallen, the ground slopes gently away northwards and the soil clearly improves. Here on this more charitable earth rise the splendid woodlands of robust oak and tall beech with the usual undergrowth of gleaming hollies. The woodlands each cover many acres, and round their boundaries following the irregular shapes of the ancient coppices can still be clearly seen the ditches and banks dug by mediaeval woodsmen. Useful they still are topped by modern fences, for where ancient trees have decayed considerable areas have been replanted, so that the woods still follow the tradition of centuries ago.

Charles II took a deep interest in the maintenance of the Forest, and he also found there a means of rewarding those for whom his shaky finances could produce no monetary benefit. In *State Papers Domestic* of 1664 appears an order of this nature:

> We are graciously pleased, upon the humble petition of Winifred Wells, one of the Maids of Honour to our dearest Consort and Queen, to give unto her the benefit of the said underwoods.

The underwoods in question were valued at £1,292, a substantial sum, but from Pepys' *Diary* it can be discovered that Winifred Wells deserved compensation for an unfortunate incident which had befallen her:

> At a ball at Court, a child was dropped by one of the ladies in dancing but nobody knew who, it being taken up by somebody in

11 St Catherine's Hill
12 The Itchen near Winchester

> a handkerchief. The next morning all the Ladies of Honour appeared early at Court for their vindication, so that nobody could tell whose this mischance should be. But it seems Mrs Wells fell sick that afternoon, and hath disappeared ever since, so that it is concluded that it was hers.

A few days later Pepys makes a further reference to this *contretemps*, but it is perhaps too indelicate to repeat in these pages. Anyhow, since Mrs Wells was one of the King's mistresses, she deserved compensation for any inconvenience she had been caused—as the papers would nowadays put it.

To return to the New Forest: it is reckoned now to cover an area of 92,395 acres, of which 64,737 are Crown lands and the remainder privately owned. These figures can mean little to most of us, except to make it clear that the Forest covers a very large area indeed. I have found no figures to show how much is woodland and how much open heathland, but I would suppose that the area of the latter is far greater than that of the former, for on the western side towards the Avon valley there are many thousands of acres which are as bleak and sterile as Dartmoor.

Gilpin divides the views obtained in the Forest into three categories, 'amusing, beautiful and picturesque'. We have perhaps become too insensitive, too unaccustomed to contemplating and dissecting prospects, to understand the distinction of these subtleties quite clearly, but it would seem that under the first heading came the views enjoyed near the coast where the waters of the Solent could be seen through the trees with the hills of the Isle of Wight beyond. They failed to qualify for either of the other two epithets, since 'the distant coast exhibits too long a curtain of Hampshire'.

'Picturesque' was, of course, a word much in use at the period when Gilpin was writing, and many a landowner was desperately trying to convert the simple grassland of his park into the likeness of a romantic scene painted by such artists as Salvator Rosa and other devotees of the picturesque landscape. In the New Forest nature had obligingly produced the scenes which landowners were at such pains to create artificially. 'Beautiful' views were presumably those which did not make the grade for either of the other two categories, and consisted principally of grass swards, or 'lawns' as Gilpin calls them, lying amongst the ancient trees.

The Forest, then, covers the heart of the area described in this chapter, and we will now make a perambulation of the outer districts, which in places are far from beautiful or romantic. Let us start at Totton, which lies at the head of Southampton Water. Let us start here but not pause, for it is an ugly and congested place, and we will quickly take a small road which leads in a south-westerly direction to the village of Eling, which lies close to the edge of the Water.

Having crossed an estuary which provides admirable harbourage for small sailing craft, one is confronted by a highly welcome survival from the past, a tollgate, and it seems that it is this gate and the sixpence one gladly pays to pass through it, that enables Eling to retain its complete integrity. Were it far from urban sprawls, it would not perhaps call for particular mention, but in its position so close to Totton and Southampton it seems miraculous to pass so suddenly into a country village.

The ground rises on the south side of the estuary, and on this modest elevation stands the church. The position is romantic, with the churchyard sloping down to a wide meadow bordering Southampton Water and an unbroken view to the opposite shore, where rises all the busy paraphernalia of the docks and of the shipping which makes Southampton one of the greatest ports in the country. Even the background of the inevitable concomitants of a thriving commercial town, factories, gasworks, chimneys, pylons, and so forth, softened to the eye by distance, melt together into a strangely exciting picture. The church itself is less remarkable than its site, and has sadly suffered from excessive restoration in 1863, but the arcades of the nave with arches supported on octagonal piers, and the fine chancel arch, date basically from the thirteenth century.

Continuing southward parallel to Southampton Water one passes through a pleasant country of meadows and copses and much hedgerow timber, but although it appears serene there is a somewhat sinister air about this area. It is as if one were visiting someone in the death cell. Alive today, but dead tomorrow, or is there to be a reprieve? Already the tall chimneys of the Marchwood Power Station suddenly appear stabbing far into the air above the trees, while further south the vast oil refinery of Fawley, in spite of the curtain of evergreen trees which has been planted round it, inevitably dominates the area where it is sited.

Before reaching the latter, a small road hugging the coastline passes through the little town of Hythe. The beauties of the place are perhaps modest, but there are a few pretty houses in the narrow, twisting main street, and the long pier stretching out for more than a third of a mile over the shallow waters into the deep channel has an agreeable nineteenth-century air.

At Fawley a conglomeration of housing estates has grown round the Refinery, and there is little here to please the eye except the church, which has great quality. It stands opposite the main gate into the Refinery, and was badly damaged during the last war. This was, as it turned out, greatly to its advantage, for in the course of restoration it was possible to eliminate the crowded embellishment of pews, encaustic tiles and decorations which had encumbered it since the nineteenth century. Now in its rather austere beauty, with its twelfth-century arcades, stout arches supporting the curiously placed south tower, and stone-paved floor, the church must look much as when it was built nearly 800 years ago. It is strange to emerge from the tranquillity of the church to hear the hum of machinery, and to see the tall flares, chimneys and oil containers of the huge refinery beyond the highway.

South of Fawley a road leads down to Hillhead and the long shingle beach which terminates in the promontory on which stands Calshot Castle, one of Henry VIII's coastal defences. A closely packed line of beach huts extends along the shingle shore, and various unsightly structures encroach on the Tudor fortifications of the Castle, but the Hampshire County Council has an admirable plan to develop the latter as a recreational centre.

Further west the country seems to lose the menaced air which exists so strongly in the neighbourhood of Southampton Water, and the narrow road which winds along the coast past Lepe, with its row of coastguards' cottages, seems unthreatened by building and suffers only from an excess of summer traffic. The road turns northward and passes through the Exbury estate with its avenues and well-kept hedges; the garden, famous for its rhododendrons and azaleas, is occasionally open to the public in the spring.

From the agreeably bosky country round Exbury the road mounts to the wide area of Beaulieu Heath, which Cobbett described as 'as barren as it is possible for land to be'. It is, indeed, one of the bleakest spaces of the Forest, with not a tree to break the expanse of heather which stretches away to the east till the view is closed by a distant prospect of the chimneys and pylons of the Fawley Refinery. The road descends from this austere landscape to the little town of Beaulieu, which lies at the point where the long winding estuary of the Beaulieu river narrows to a wide stream.

The Abbey was founded in this tranquil place, which deserved its name of Bellus Locus, in 1204 by King John—an unlikely patron for a religious house—and became a place of great importance and size. At the Dissolution the huge church and a large part of the other buildings were demolished, leaving however the Refectory, which now serves as the parish church, and the impressive fourteenth-century gatehouse which is incorporated into Palace House, with a number of vaulted rooms of the same period. Much of the house was rebuilt in the late nineteenth century by Sir Arthur Blomfield, who fairly successfully harmonised the new work he designed with the mediaeval.

Amongst these ancient stone walls are arranged all the attractions which bring thousands upon thousands of tourists to the place in the course of the year. The Motor Museum, the coach and car parks, the restaurants, souvenir kiosks, teas and toilets, a model railway, all are efficiently laid out to cope with the throngs of visitors. When there were only ruins to inspect the numbers were no doubt minimal; now they are astronomical, so that the pleasure provided is vastly increased, and one is no doubt wrong to feel that Bellus Locus no longer deserves its name.

The church lies a little apart from all the fun, and is a plain, rather barn-like but imposing building. It has served as the parish church since the sixteenth century, almost ever since the abbey church was demolished after the Dissolution. Owing to its original purpose as the Refectory it is orientated north to south with the altar at the south end. The principal feature of the church is the pulpit on the west side. The stair up to it is built in the thickness of the wall with an arcade of six small Gothic arches supported on pairs of slender black marble pillars which mount with the rise of the steps to the pulpit, which projects like a balcony into the church. The parapet is clearly nineteenth-century, but the massive carved support in the shape of an inverted cone is said to date from the fourteenth century.

Three miles south of Beaulieu on the west bank of the river, which is here within a short distance of the mouth of the estuary, is the curious little place known as Bucklers Hard. It consists now of two ranges of red-brick cottages with a grass sward between them. The buildings are stepped down the gentle slope leading to the placid tidal waters of the river, which winds between low banks with long sweeps of the Exbury oakwoods on the further shore. The north row is terminated by the Master Builder's House, a fine little building of eighteenth-century date with a pedimented doorway.

This short street was the creation of the second Duke of Montagu, and was the first part of an ambitious scheme to create here a town and docks to receive the produce from the Island of Lucia, which was his property. The plan collapsed, however, and neither town nor docks were built, so that these two rows of trim houses are all there is now to show for an ambitious enterprise. But if commercially the port failed to materialise, as a shipbuilding yard the place thrived for several centuries and warships of considerable size were constructed on this deep-water estuary from the oak timber which was so conveniently at hand in the Forest. As late as 1800 HMS *Spencer*, 1,917 tons and carrying a crew of 600 men, was built here, but the most famous ship from these yards was the *Agamemnon*, of 1781, which was commanded for several years by Nelson and took part in the battles of both Copenhagen and Trafalgar.

The men-of-war have disappeared from these gentle waters, and their place has been taken by sailing boats. The estuary vies with

Hamble as a place for yachts to moor and to visit, and since it is remote from great towns, it has more seclusion than the latter.

To the north-west of Beaulieu lie some of the most beautiful and romantic areas of the Forest. The main roads centring on Lyndhurst with their wide grass verges bordered by deep woodland seem like drives through a wild private park, the sort of park that Humphry Repton would have approved of, with trees growing at random where Nature planted them and with thickets of holly and hawthorn forming an undergrowth amongst the oaks and beeches. From the highways smaller roads and tracks lead away invitingly through the trees into the heart of the woodlands.

It is an area to enjoy nature rather than architecture, but although the few villages and little towns—Lyndhurst, I think, has the latter stature—are not very distinguished there are a number of churches worth visiting. Two or three miles to the north-west of Lyndhurst is Minstead, for example. From the small green, which forms the centre of this scattered collection of houses, a lane leads up a short hill to this most curious little building. Were it not for the brick tower of 1774, it would appear on approach to be purely domestic, an ancient farmhouse perhaps, to which dormers, gables and additions had been made in random manner during the centuries. This indeed has been the process, the local seventeenth- and eighteenth-century builders who transformed an early Gothic church into something more up-to-date being more conversant with domestic than with ecclesiastical building. The charmingly confused interior with its lopsided chancel arch, two galleries, one above the other, cosy private pews—one with fireplace—double-decker pulpit, all give the impression of local carpenters, with much oak to hand, carrying out their solid, sensible work without knowledge of architectural developments in the world beyond the confines of the Forest. In the churchyard are the graves of Sir Arthur Conan Doyle and his wife, who lived in the parish.

There could hardly be a greater contrast than that between this unselfconscious little conventicle and the large, nineteenth-century church at Lyndhurst. The latter stands in a commanding position on a high bank at the top of the town, and is also a very commanding building. There is nothing modest or bucolic about it, it is the epitome of the Church Militant and prosperous. It was begun in 1860, from the design of William White, and is constructed in a vivid scarlet brick diversified with bands of yellow brick with a border of blue and red headers. There is a lavish use of stonework, and at the west end a tall steeple. The passing of a century seems to have had no mellowing effect on these durable building materials. The interior, in the same materials, is spacious and very high, with carved figures supporting the trusses of the roof. The arcades of the two aisles are supported on brick piers surrounded by clusters of what appear to be Purbeck marble shafts, but which, I very much fear, are in fact iron pipes. This would hardly seem to be an example of that 'truthfulness' in art which was loudly advocated by the Victorians.

The shell of the church, then, is perhaps not particularly appealing, but it contains a number of really beautiful examples of the crafts of the period. It is an outstanding example of how far more sensitive and attractive was the art of the Pre-Raphaelite School than the conventional architecture of the day. There are stained-glass windows by William Morris, Burne-Jones, Philip Webb, Ford Madox Brown and Rossetti. There are also later ones by Kemp, Clayton and Bell, and Powell. In the Baptistry is a moving monument designed by Samuel Pepys Cockerell to his wife, who died at the age of 23 in 1880. A mosaic panel of a sun in splendour forms a background to the recumbent marble figure, and a forged-iron rail in a flowing *Art Nouveau* manner encloses a semi-circular platform decorated with flowers. More conventional than the foregoing is the large mural painted by Frederick Leighton below the east window representing the parable of the Wise and the Foolish Virgins. Lyndhurst church, in fact, is not one to be neglected by those interested in the arts of the nineteenth century.

The villages of the Forest have shown an inclination to develop in a position remote from their parish church. This is the case to some degree at Minstead; it is very much the case at both Brockenhurst and Boldre. Both have beautiful and ancient churches charmingly sited in bosky surroundings well away from the centre they serve.

13 *In the New Forest*

St Peter's, Brockenhurst, claims to be the oldest church in the Forest and, since a church is recorded as existing on this site in the Domesday Survey of 1086, the claim is probably justified. No doubt Saxon remains are incorporated in the existing building, but the earliest feature to be seen is the Norman south doorway with its fine, dog-tooth moulding. The chancel was built in the thirteenth century, the tower in the eighteenth, and the north aisle, clearly with an eye on economy, early in the nineteenth. But in spite of these various dates it presents a mellow and harmonious whole. The splendid yew tree in the churchyard may well, I think, have been planted when the church was built.

Scattered building has occurred all about the Boldre area, but the immediate surroundings of the church are completely pastoral, a perfect setting of woods and meadows. The church is long and low with a robust tower, fourteenth-century below and seventeenth-century above, standing at the south-east corner of the nave. The interior is impressive, with a robust and rather rustic arcade to the south aisle, and a more sophisticated and graceful twelfth-century arcade dating from a century later to the north. In this mediaeval setting the finely coloured east window designed by Alan Young and erected in 1967 is extremely effective. On the wall of the north aisle is a monument to William Gilpin, whose writings have already been mentioned. He died in 1804, having been Vicar of Boldre for 30 years. With the money he earned with his books on Forest scenery and the cult of the picturesque he founded a free school in the parish. Seldom can literary earnings have been put to a better or more lasting use. It was in this area that Captain Marryat set Arnwood, the home of his *Children of the New Forest*.

A short way to the south of Boldre the romantic country of the Forest ends, and houses are inclined to predominate over trees; but it is possible to follow a small road close to the river Lymington down to the town of the same name. The river is of modest size, but as it nears the coast it widens out into an estuary, a modest replica of the Beaulieu river, and at high tide forms a handsome sheet of water; at low tide, when the shallow waters recede and mud is revealed, the effect is less impressive. At the point where the stream widens out

14 *The Beaulieu river at Beaulieu*

there is, as at Eling, a charming anachronistic toll bridge.

The town of Lymington is the largest and the most attractive town in the Forest area, and has great character and charm. The High Street, of ample width, mounts the steep slope from the water towards the church which, with its square stone tower surmounted by a massive cupola, stands nobly on the summit of the rise. The tower forms a handsome eye-catcher at the top of the street, which curves round it and continues on a slightly diminished scale to the western outskirts of the town.

It cannot be said that all the buildings lining this fine street are beautiful—indeed, far from it—but the very mixture of architecture from seventeenth to twentieth century provides interest and variety, although some of the latest have replaced structures of greater distinction. The church has made its effect with its tower: the body of the building is not of great interest. Although it is mediaeval in form and incorporates some early work, it is the alterations of the eighteenth century which provide the principal character. Plain galleries are supported on twin Tuscan colums, and plaster vaulting covers the nave and chancel: the transformation was serviceable rather than lavish.

To the west of Lymington building is spreading fast and becomes ever more intense as one nears Christchurch, but within this area there are a number of buildings of interest. At Milford, for example, the church is well worth visiting, although modern housing now joins the old village to the buildings on the coast. Agreeably secluded in its well-kept churchyard, it is low, spreading and spacious and dates principally from the late thirteenth century, but at the west end parts of the original Norman church have been incorporated. It is surprising to find churches so large as this, and also those at Brockenhurst and Boldre, in districts where in the Middle Ages the population must have been scarce and scattered: now, with a surge of buildings beginning to surround them, they are no longer too large for their congregations.

South of Milford a long promontory stretches out into the Solent and on the extremity stands Hurst Castle, another of Henry VIII's coastal defences. It was to this secure fortress that Charles I was brought as a prisoner from Carisbrooke on the last day of November, 1648. Thence on 17 December he was taken to Windsor, and a few weeks later to St James's Palace to await his trial.

From Milford a minor road passing close to the coast leads to Milton. From the length where it runs by the shore there is a fine view across the water to the jagged range of the Needles and the lighthouse on their furthest point. These rocks mark the end of the long, protecting bulwark formed by the high downs of the Isle which shelter much of this coastal area from the south-west gales. To the west of Milford, however, the coast is exposed to the full blast of the Atlantic winds, and the few trees and bushes that can live against it are stunted into strange geometrical shapes.

Amongst the housing estates which cover the area further west there is little to detain those in search of beauty or antiquity, though some may care to pause and shed a tear at Highcliffe. Here still stands, engulfed in housing, the Gothic castle built by Lord Stuart de Rothesay between the years 1830 and 1834. The architect was W. Donthorne, but into the fabric was incorporated late mediaeval stonework brought from Les Andelys in France. The fifteenth century and the nineteenth may not have united in perfect harmony, but nevertheless the resulting composition was romantic and dramatic in spite of its absurdity. Now it is derelict and forlorn, since two fires have lately broken out in the empty fabric and at the time of writing this ruined folly is as securely defended by barricades of barbed wire as the Sleeping Beauty by the thickets of thorns.

Probably one should not enlarge in a short book of this sort on a building that may have ceased to exist before these words are in print, but, rejecting prudence, I propose to continue on the subject. On Lord Stuart's death the house was inherited by his daughter Louisa, Lady Waterford, who divided her life between Highcliffe and her house in Northumberland. She and her sister Lady Canning are the subjects of Augustus Hare's *Two Noble Lives*, and now it is the quiet domestic life of Lady Waterford rather than the animated political life of her sister which is of the greater interest.

Lord Stuart, who was perhaps the most eccentric ambassador the British Government ever sent to Paris, chose a time when his wife was safely occupied elsewhere in looking after an invalid father to carry on his gigantic building operations without her knowledge. Augustus Hare quotes a letter written by Lady Stuart to her husband on returning to Highcliffe to find that the neat villa she had left had grown into a vast, sprawling castle. She was highly critical of both her husband and the architect, and wrote sharply:

> The best room is tolerable, but in all the mass of building to have squeezed up such wretched bedrooms stamps him [Donthorne] as totally unfit to plan a house. . . . When I think it is for *this* we are *ruined* . . . I wish the whole thing had fallen over the cliff.

Neither financial consideration, nor his wife's despair, appear to have moved Lord Stuart very deeply, and he and his architect continued to embellish the building for several years to come.

One of Lady Waterford's benefactions was the building of the white stone church of St Mark, which dates from 1845. It is reached by a private road beneath an avenue of ilex and lime trees which leaves the main road opposite the twin lodges which once guarded the drive to the Castle, and are a survival from the house designed by Robert Adam for Lord Bute, which stood near the edge—too near, as eventually became apparent—of the cliff. It is now rather a sad little structure with modern building pressing close round the churchyard, but the spirit of Lady Waterford seems still to linger there, perpetuated by several of her oil paintings which hang on the walls—for she was a talented artist. There are monuments, too, in a not very graceful Gothic style, to her and to her parents.

She described to Augustus Hare the building of the church of which she laid the foundation stone. 'The bell was brought from Russia by my father and mother, and has (as all Russian bells) some silver in it to improve the tone. . . . The window over the communion table was my own idea and execution, the ornamentation my sister's. . . . The evergreen oak and lime avenue near the church was planted at that time.'

In the churchyard a handsome marble sarcophagus covers, or perhaps contains, the remains of the mother of Gordon Selfridge, the founder of the Oxford Street store, who rented the Castle for some years. Next to the sarcophagus a more modest marble monument marks the grave of his wife, and nearby a small plain headstone his own grave, this descending sequence indicating the decline, indeed the collapse, of the Selfridge fortune.

Leaving these melancholy evidences of former splendour one can follow the busy, trafficky road into Christchurch. It is not a town of architectural distinction, or of charm, in spite of its agreeable situation on a rise above the junction of the Avon and the Stour, and close to the almost landlocked harbour through which their waters pass to the sea, but in the Priory it has the most splendid ecclesiastical building in the County after Winchester Cathedral and Romsey Abbey. The long, grey, stone structure stands on the highest part of the ridge between the rivers, and public gardens with several eighteenth-century houses in rosy brick rising from emerald-green turf form a perfect setting for the distinguished architecture of the Priory.

It is a complex building of several dates, but the nave and transepts date from the years on either side of 1100 and were begun by Flambard—this being one of the more meritorious works of this somewhat unscrupulous bishop—while the graceful Gothic chancel and Lady Chapel date from the fifteenth century, and the tower at the west end was built in the same century. The long flight of semicircular arches in the nave with the triforium above are splendid examples of Norman building, and the interlaced arcading on the exterior of the north transept is fine work of the same period. The late Gothic of the remainder of the Priory is particularly delicate and graceful, and reaches its epitome in the small chapels on either side of the choir. This is a highly simplified description, but is perhaps adequate to encourage a close inspection of this beautiful building.

The Priory contains a number of interesting monuments, but a particularly poignant one is to the poet Shelley. It is the work of Henry Weekes, and shows the drowned body of the poet lying amidst rocks, as if just washed ashore, while his wife supports his head and gazes intently at him. The monument was refused for Westminster Abbey, and was erected here in 1854 by his son who lived at Boscombe. Not far away in the churchyard of St Peter's, Bournemouth, Mary Shelley is buried and the poet's heart, which was snatched from the funeral pyre by Trelawny, is buried with her.

The Priory is not the only building of merit and antiquity in Christchurch: there is also the ruined Castle which stands to the north of the Priory close to the banks of the mill stream. Its interest is perhaps more archaeological than general, since little survives beyond the walls of the twelfth-century hall, but its architectural importance lies in the fact that it is one of the very few survivals of domestic buildings of this early period.

Christchurch merges into Bournemouth. I do not propose to guide you into this salubrious resort, not owing to any prejudice against it —for it has much to recommend it—but its pleasant character needs no particular description. I might mention that amidst the predominantly nineteenth-century architecture several good modern buildings can be seen looking perhaps a little self-conscious in their highly conservative surroundings, but no doubt they will soon settle down. Instead we will turn northward and streak up the valley of the Avon, which on this stretch is less picturesque than might be expected, and pass through Ringwood and continue for another couple of miles to Ellingham.

A church without a village is rather rare, but this is the case at Ellingham, where there is not so much as a hamlet to account for its presence. But there it stands, charmingly secluded at the end of a *cul-de-sac* near the entrance to Somerley Park. However, its isolation has not led to neglect, for it is admirably maintained and has been so for many decades. A good deal of late nineteenth-century restoration was carried out here, but without that harshness which was prevalent at the period, so that it is not easily distinguished from the original thirteenth-century work. It is built of large, roughly squared stones, but the porch was added in 1720, and the west end, surprisingly enough, has a neat classical façade in brick with stone quoins of 1747. The interior is as attractive as the exterior, with its rather rustic, fifteenth-century wooden screen to the chancel and canopied family pew, partly nineteenth century, on the north side. An unexpected feature is a splendidly carved, early eighteenth-century reredos at the west end, which was moved from the east end during the restoration of 1884. It consists of Corinthian pilasters supporting a pediment within which delicate carving of flowers and drapery in the manner of Grinling Gibbons surrounds a painting of the Judgment Day.

In the churchyard and near the porch a stone tomb bears the names of Dame Alice Lisle and her daughter. Alice Lisle was sentenced to death by burning by Judge Jeffries for having sheltered two fugitives from Monmouth's army after Sedgemoor. After numerous petitions this brutal sentence was changed to decapitation, which took place in The Square at Winchester on 2 September 1685. The house where Alice Lisle lived and provided this disastrous shelter was Moyles Court, which lies a mile to the east of the Avon valley within the borders of the Forest. It is a charming early Restoration house built in brick, with tall chimney stacks and a high, tiled roof. A number of houses of this type were erected about England at this active period of country house building. It is now a preparatory school and, although not open to the public, can be well seen from the highway.

From these places of melancholy memory the A 388 continues northward up the valley and crosses the Avon into Fordingbridge. It is not, it must be owned, an attractive town. It is largely nineteenth century and its narrow streets are singularly unsuited to the heavy traffic produced by a junction of several main roads. It has, however, quite an interesting church on the far south-west outskirts of the town, where a number of rather picturesque cottages still exist. This was probably the original nucleus of the place before development took place near the junction of the roads and the bridge. The dominating feature of the exterior is the fine battlemented tower on the north side, dating probably from the fifteenth century, and of the surprisingly light interior the principal ornament is the splendid roof of the north chapel, in which wooden angels support the hammer-beams.

Another object of interest in the town must be mentioned: the Augustus John Memorial. I seem to remember that there was controversy about the site where it was to be erected, and this was not very happily solved by placing it in a corner of the Children's Recreation Ground on the east bank of the river. It consists of a life-sized bronze figure of the artist raised on a plain stone base. He is represented as a rather shambling figure in baggy trousers and shirt, and with bare feet. His face is drawn and haggard, and he has none of that handsome swagger which he maintained until well past middle age. I find it rather a sad memorial of a remarkable man.

To the west of Fordingbridge lies the area known as the Martin peninsula, that strange, wedge-shaped piece of country lying between Wiltshire and Dorset. As I have mentioned in the Introduction, the three parishes of Damerham, Martin and Rockbourne were added to Hampshire in 1895 in the interests of simplifying county boundaries which up to that time had been extremely complex and involved. It cannot be said that Hampshire thereby gained any country of great beauty, for the western part at least is austere without being grand, though it appears to be good open farming land. Through the peninsula, however, run two small streams both following a south-easterly course towards the Avon, the Allen and Sweatfords Water, the latter rather a brook than a stream. In these shallow valleys where the bleakness of the uplands gives way to silver willows and green meadows lie the three villages.

The first of these, Damerham, is so scattered that it can hardly be called a village, but its church stands well, remote on a rise above the valley surrounded by dark yew trees. However, since it is one of the very few churches in the county which is kept locked, I should be rash to encourage a visit. Martin is definitely a village, and a charming one too, with many thatched cottages standing behind grass verges along the valley road. The church stands on the north side of the road, and although it was rather ruthlessly Victorianised much of the thirteenth- and fourteenth-century work survives.

A stretch of the northern boundary of the parish, and thus also the boundary between Hampshire and Wiltshire, is formed by the huge earthwork known as Grim's Ditch. It extends for many miles, enclosing altogether an area of 16 square miles. In the lengths where it is well-preserved it consists of twin banks, 50 feet wide with a ditch six feet deep between them. Excavations suggest that it dates

15 *Lymington church*
16 *Breamore church*

15 (above) *Lymington church*

16 *Breamore church*

from the Middle Bronze Age.

From the Allen valley a small road leads over the uplands and so down into the valley of Sweatfords Water and to Rockbourne. This is quite a considerable village, containing not only pretty cottages but also a number of middle-sized houses, houses with drives and gates. The church stands high above the village on the north flank of the valley and is not only difficult to find but also rather difficult of access—but a visit is well worth the climb. The exterior is not very impressive for the church is dug deeply into the hillside, but the interior with a long arcade of Transitional arches between the nave and the north aisle has considerable style, and much thirteenth-century work has survived the restoration of 1893.

In the chancel are a number of charming early nineteenth-century monuments to the Coote family (most of the males bore the Christian name of Eyre), who lived at West Park in the parish. The house has now been demolished, but the column erected in memory of General Sir Eyre Coote, the famous Indian general, still stands as a landmark on a high point of the park. Below the church are the extensive remains of manorial buildings dating from the thirteenth to the seventeenth century. There is a huge fifteenth-century barn, and a chapel building with a cinquefoil entrance door dating from two centuries earlier, and other massive stone structures forming rather unusual features of a large farmyard. It is pleasant to see these ancient buildings still put to the use for which they were built many centuries ago.

Turning back towards the Hampshire mainland, one leaves this open area and can follow a deep, narrow lane through beautifully undulating and wooded country to Breamore on the east side of the Avon valley. Like Rockbourne, the village contains a number of attractive eighteenth-century houses, the sort of houses of which Horace Walpole wrote: 'I perceive there is peculiar to us middling houses, how snug they are!' But it is the church and Breamore House which are of particular beauty and interest.

The church stands on the edge of Breamore Park in a setting of tall cedars and other evergreens, and is the finest example in the country of a Saxon church. It is built of uncut flints with quoins of long and

17 Christchurch Priory: the south choir aisle

short stone work of typical pre-Conquest style, and the squat central bell tower is also of that period. The chancel was rebuilt in the fourteenth century, and the present chancel arch replaced the Saxon arch shortly after this period.

Within the porch is the object of the greatest interest in the church, the Saxon rood over the south door. The porch itself was erected in the middle of the twelfth century, and the upper part, which originally formed a small chapel covering the rood, from the fifteenth. It has been sadly mutilated, but the strangely sculptured figure of Christ on the Cross, with Our Lady and St John on either side, and the hand of God projecting from a cloud, are clear, while a frescoed landscape background with the hanging figure of Judas is dimly visible. There is much else of interest in the church, particularly the Saxon windows with their splays both outside and in; while the eighteenth century has contributed a collection of ten hatchments appertaining to the Hulse family which hang on the walls below the tower.

Breamore House stands on the sloping park a few hundred yards to the north of the church. It was completed in 1583, and is an imposing example of brick architecture with a symmetrical E-shaped south font facing southward across the park to the cedars round the churchyard. In the middle of the last century it was very seriously damaged by fire, but was restored so far as possible to its original appearance. It is open to the public throughout the summer.

Breamore lies at the base of a great area of downland which rises to the north-west of the village and the park. Lanes lead up on to these windy uplands, and those who enjoy a romantic prospect will be rewarded for a certain amount of walking for the tracks are apt to peter out. To the north Clearbury Hill, with its crest of trees planted within a circle of earthworks, rises against the sky, and to the north-west the pale green of downland turf is broken by the dark form of Great Yews, a rather sinister group of ancient trees, the remains of a woodland which once covered a considerable area. To the east, between the slopes of the downs the eye is carried to the dense woodlands of the New Forest, and to the south and the west the view stretches away into Dorset and Wiltshire.

A mile or two across the valley of the Avon from Breamore stand the church and house of Hale, where in place of Saxon and Elizabethan architecture that of the eighteenth century predominates. For this was the house of that highly individual architect Thomas Archer who made drastic alterations to both house and church about 1715. The house, approached by a long double avenue of lime trees, now consists of a handsome porticoed central block flanked by a pavilion on either side of the forecourt. It is difficult to disentangle the work of Thomas Archer from that of Henry Holland, who made alterations in 1770, but the pilastered bay in the centre of the south side seems typical of Archer's style. The house is open to the public on several days in the week during the late summer and early autumn.

The church, which lies on the steep slope of the valley below the house still retains unaltered the classical dress in which Archer clothed the existing small mediaeval building and to which he added transepts. The Victorians, who could never leave even an eighteenth-century church alone, made singularly unfortunate alterations to the windows. In the church there are three splendid classical monuments, of which that to Thomas Archer himself is the finest. It dates from 1739, although he did not die till four years later, so no doubt he made his own design in order to ensure he was suitably commemorated in death. The position of the church is particularly attractive, high above the Avon with a prospect through an opening in the woods of the gently moving river winding through the water meadows.

From these Arcadian scenes the B 3078 leads in a south-easterly direction close to the county boundary to Cadnam, a junction of many roads. Here to the north and east the magic of the Forest ceases, and the A 31 which crosses the whole of Hampshire leads away to Romsey, and so also into Chapter Three.

CHAPTER THREE

The Test valley and High Hampshire

The area covered by this chapter is the north-west section of the county, through which passes the river Test flowing down from beyond Whitchurch and being joined a little way along its course by the much smaller river Anton which rises north of Andover. All this area is chalk country, the familiar Hampshire chalk, except for the alluvial soil in the valleys of these two rivers. But for convenience of descriptions we will overlap a little on to the clay country in the south and start our excursion from Romsey. This will fill in the comparatively narrow strip of country lying between the area covered by Chapter One and the county boundary on the west.

Romsey, as a whole, is not a beautiful town, and in this it is a disappointment, as one would expect that a place containing one of the finest Norman buildings in the south of England, a broad river, and a romantic park surrounding a handsome classical house on its south side, must have great charm. But, alas, the main streets are singularly lacking in architectural distinction, and there is little to delay one, except for a glance at the statue of Lord Palmerston brooding over the Market Place, until one comes to the noble grey form of the Abbey set back from the road to Stockbridge on the west side of the town.

The exterior of the Abbey with its low tower and massive walls has the severe, almost defensive appearance which is a characteristic of Norman buildings, but the pair of semi-circular chapels with their graceful round-topped windows, which are in the angles between the transepts and the presbytery, give an indication of the beauty within. The entrance is by a modern porch on the north side of the nave, and before one rise the superb flights of round-topped arches mounting one above the other to the triforium and clerestory of the nave, presbytery and transepts. The greater part of this structure dates from the 50 years following 1120, though on the south side there is a stretch of eleventh-century walling, while the two west bays of the nave and the west end were built in the thirteenth century.

This is a general indication of the principal dates of building, but it is less dates than the beauty of the architecture, so strong and yet so graceful, which impress, and the variety of designs on the single theme of the semi-circular arch which is here displayed. The slender piers supporting arches with dog-tooth decoration set within the clustered pillars and moulded arches of the triforium, and the plainer triple arches of the clerestory produce an effect of extreme richness.

The cloisters which were originally in the angle of the south transept and aisle have disappeared, but the south doorway is a particularly splendid example of Norman work, and close to it, on the west-facing wall of the transept, is a remarkable rood, carved in stone and dating probably from the first half of the eleventh century. The figure of Christ is shown as living, with the head erect and the eyes open, and not in death as is more usual.

Down a *cul-de-sac* on the opposite side of the Stockbridge road to the Abbey is a building known as King John's House. It is built of stone and flint and dates apparently from the thirteenth century, but is unlikely to have been used by that monarch as a hunting box. It consists of two rooms on the ground floor with the main hall on the first floor, which now contains a collection of Romseyana. Against the west wall of the building is a little, timber-framed cottage, dating probably from three centuries later. Together they make an attractive and unexpected group set as they are behind dull late nineteenth-century houses lining the street.

Broadlands, on the south side of the town, where the by-pass skirts the park wall, is not open to the public, but from the road bridge crossing the Test there is a romantic view along the river as it winds through the park with the house fronted by a tall, late eighteenth-century portico rising on the east bank. The appearance of the house is the work of Henry Holland, who made alterations in 1788, and at the same time decorated the three beautiful rooms overlooking the river.

The house was the home of Lord Palmerston, the famous Victorian Prime Minister, who died in office in 1865, no doubt to the Queen's considerable relief, as their relations had never been warm. After his death Victoria wrote of him: 'He had many valuable qualities, though many bad ones . . . I never liked him.' The present Queen and the Duke of Edinburgh spent part of their honeymoon at Broadlands, which is now the property of Lord Mountbatten.

A famous son of Romsey was Sir William Petty, who was born in the town in 1625. He was one of those brilliant and versatile characters who are inclined to achieve less than those whose talents follow a single course. William Petty was philosopher, politician, administrator, inventor, scientist, mathematician, indeed there were few directions, except in the visual arts, where he did not make useful contributions. He was also a poet, and John Evelyn wrote of him: 'There is not a better Latin poet living.' He is perhaps chiefly remembered now for his inventions, of which the first duplicating apparatus and an unsinkable boat with a double keel were the best-known. Early in his career he achieved considerable fame by reviving the corpse of one Anne Green, who had been hanged for murder and pronounced dead. It is not recorded that he ever attempted a similar, rather controversial, experiment again. He died in 1687 and was buried in Romsey Abbey, where there is a monument to him erected in the last century.

Two miles west of Romsey, in country where the clay and sandy soil is more akin to that in the New Forest to the south than to the chalk country to the north, is Embly Park, now a school, the house in which Florence Nightingale spent much of her youth. Her father bought the estate in 1826 when Florence was six years old, and here she led the aimless existence of an unmarried young woman at that period. In 1852 she wrote a novel which was never published, called *Cassandra*, and in it she describes the dreary, stifling daily round in the average upper-class home. The mornings were spent 'sitting round a table in the drawing room, looking at prints, doing worsted work, and reading little books', and the afternoons were passed 'taking a little drive'. The lack of purpose in their lives often made women physically ill, she declared.

However, two years later the Crimean War broke out, and Florence Nightingale was soon set on the career which brought her fame. She died in 1910 at the age of 90, and was buried in the churchyard at East Wellow, in which parish Embly stands. The simple little church, with a shingled bell turret at the west end, dates principally from the thirteenth century, with a south aisle added in the sixteenth century. There must have been many similar churches in Hampshire, until the nineteenth-century passion for improvement either demolished them or altered them beyond recognition. East Wellow, however, has one unusual feature, its wall paintings. These are apparently contemporary with the structure, and are partly patterned decoration, and partly figures—St Christopher and what is said to be the murder of Thomas à Becket—but a considerable exercise of the imagination is required to comprehend these scenes.

North of the A 27 chalk once more comes to the surface in the long ridge of Dean Hill. The greater part lies in Wiltshire, but the east end is in Hampshire, and the long slope, dark with a thick growth of yew trees, is a complete contrast to the rather flat country we have just passed through with its oaks and pine trees and much pontecum undergrowth. At the foot of the hill on the north side is the hamlet of East Dean (West Dean is across the boundary in Wiltshire). It is an uninteresting little place except for its appealing church, which must be one of the smallest in the county. It has a little belfry containing a single bell and a primitive wooden gallery across the west end. It is otherwise entirely unadorned.

A mile or two to the north is the village of West Tytherley where, amidst bosky and tranquil surroundings, the community of Owenite Socialists was founded in 1841 in a building known as Harmony Hall. Robert Owen, the founder and president of the community, was a dynamic if eccentric idealist whose doctrine was that 'the natural standard of value is human labour'. In pursuance of this principle he not only denounced the ill-effects of the introduction of machinery, but went so far as to advocate the use of the spade in place of the plough. His experiment coincided with the opening of 'The Hungry Forties' when the distress and privation amongst the working classes was very great, but his well-intentioned principles were too reactionary to succeed, and the cult failed within a few years. Harmony Hall stood as a witness to a benevolent if ill-conceived enterprise until 1903, when it was demolished.

Returning to the valley of the Test, we come to the attractive village and the beautiful abbey of Mottisfont. The church and village stand on the gentle slope rising from the valley with its many streams. Much of the nave of the church dates from the twelfth century, and the splendid chancel arch with its dog-tooth decoration is of this period. The chancel itself is fifteenth-century and has a handsome, traceried east window.

The principal interest of the place, however, lies in the Abbey, which is now the property of the National Trust. It stands low in the valley, with a subsidiary stream running close beside it, while the main river is beyond a wide belt of trees to the east. Trees grow well in this damp alluvial soil, and the garden of the Abbey contains a number of planes of exceptional size. In this romantic setting of water and foliage stands the late thirteenth-century Abbey which was converted after the Dissolution into a domestic building by Lord Sandys. The main body of the house is formed out of the nave of the church, while the north transept and all to the east of the crossing was demolished. In the mid-eighteenth century the buildings which projected southward from the west end of the nave were terminated in a three-sided bay window, while the south transept was similarly treated; between them a domestic façade in brick was erected, allowing for a wide gallery behind it joining the two wings and giving access to the rooms formed in the nave.

This is roughly the plan of what may be called the *piano nobile*, and here the appearance is predominantly eighteenth-century, but at ground-floor level much of the original monastic building is to be seen, particularly in the splendid vaulting on short, robust columns beneath the western projection, and a very complete arcade in what was originally the wall of the nave. To this amalgam of the work of different centuries the twentieth has made its contribution in a mosaic by Boris Anrep in a recessed corner of the south front, and in the saloon in the south-west projection which was painted in 1938/9 by Rex Whistler. Here his inventive genius, which was so soon to be extinguished by his death during the war, is shown in its full development. The house is admirably furnished, and is still lived in by the donor, thus it retains the personal flavour which vanishes like smoke once a house is only a showpiece.

From Mottisfont the valley of the Test runs almost due north, and its picturesqueness is perhaps slightly modified by the fact that the railway and two roads, one on either side, accompany the river towards Stockbridge. How, one wonders, would the difficult problems of introducing railway lines into the countryside nowadays be solved? A century and a quarter or so ago, when a network of lines across Hampshire to Southampton appeared essential, the three river valleys, Test, Itchen and Meon, running conveniently from north to south, seemed designed by nature as sites for the railways, and only the Avon valley was fortunate enough to escape. There were no hills to negotiate, there were few buildings in these damp meadows to be acquired and demolished, and the fact that the peaceful beauty of the valleys would be disturbed may have seemed a small price to pay for the convenient service provided. Now we have become so accustomed to the sight of a railway that we almost accept it as part of the landscape, and are less distressed by it than we should be by a wide new road, and indeed with only occasional trains as opposed to a constant stream of motor traffic, the nuisance is not very great.

With these thoughts in mind one can linger with pleasure on the little road which crosses the valley halfway between Mottisfont and Stockbridge. It leaves the main road on the east side near King's Somborne, itself rather an attractive village, where the principal houses are gathered round a small green, and a little tributary to the Test runs through the eastern part of the place. The church, on the side of the green, is rather formidable. Although some thirteenth-century work survives, a deeply incised inscription on one of the pillars of the nave announces that: 'This ancient church was fully restored 1885. The ring of bells was completed in the Jubilee year of Queen Victoria, 1887.' This is no overstatement: when a structure was 'fully restored' in the late nineteenth century it would indicate that little of the original fabric would be allowed to survive without evidence of industrious rechiselling.

To return, however, to the road across the valley. It passes over bridge after bridge—the highest indeed is that of the railway, but let us forget it—some over narrow, some over wide sheets of water with sudden prospects opening between the silver willows up and down the wide, watery valley. I think there is little doubt that the Test gains the prize for the most beautiful river valley in the county.

By devious turns the road reaches the hamlet of Bossington close to which the Wallop Brook, which we shall meet again later, joins the Test, and at this point is a wide marshy area known as John of Gaunt's Deer Park lying on either side of a branch of the Test. In this well-watered soil, willow, poplar and alder thrive luxuriantly, but deer, one would suppose, would have found the park uncomfortably damp.

Two miles up the Wallop Brook is the pretty village of Broughton, where Anne Steele, the hymn-writer, was born in 1717. A tragedy befell her in her early life when her fiancé was drowned a few hours before the time fixed for the wedding, and the mournful note of the 144 hymns, 34 metrical psalms, and 50 poems which she wrote in the course of her life reflect this early reverse. She never married, and was buried in the churchyard at Broughton in 1778.

The village is particularly charming, with the stream running through meadows on the east side, and the main road conveniently away on the west so that the centre of the village, in which are many timber-framed and brick houses, is little disturbed by through traffic. The church on the east side of the street dates principally from very early in the thirteenth century, but in 1638 was almost entirely gutted by fire. The arcades to the nave, however, largely survived, but it can be seen how the capitals of some of the stout columns were calcined by the heat. A number of moulded stones, which had fallen during the fire, were worked into the flintwork of the outer walls of the chancel.

Of the two roads in the main valley which accompany the Test northward the smaller on the west keeps near the water, while the principal road on the east mounts on to rather higher ground away from the river, but both arrive within a few hundred yards of each other at opposite ends of Stockbridge. This is a place which calls for little comment. It consists of a single wide street running due east and west with a bridge over the Test at the latter end. The spacious scale of its single street is impressive, but it has not been particularly fortunate in the architecture of the buildings which border it. It has none of the trim elegance of Broad Street at Alresford, for example, where the scale is rather similar; in fact most of the houses appear to be haphazard developments of the early twentieth century, and the early nineteenth-century Grosvenor Hotel, centrally placed on the north side of the street, is one of the few buildings to present a front of any distinction to the road.

From Stockbridge we will advance in a north-westerly direction making a predominantly clockwise sweep on to the chalk uplands—partly arable, partly down—known as High Hampshire, and then southward again till we meet the areas covered in Chapters One and Four. Before mounting to the high ground which rises steeply immediately to the west of Stockbridge, we will make a short excursion up the Test valley. As further south, the railway and two roads continue along this stretch, the first of these and the principal of the second running on the east side. But in spite of these aids to transport the valley remains extremely beautiful, for the Test here broadens out into wide, lake-like expanses with many minor streams flowing through the meadows. Groups of willows and alders grow by the water, and the steep chalk hills which border the valley are largely covered with beech trees. When one climbs from this wet and sheltered valley on to the hills on either side the contrast in scene is dramatic, for the landscape is strictly utilitarian with wide arable fields with few trees to break the winds which blow across these uplands.

There are two villages in this stretch of the valley: Leckford on the east side and Longstock on the west. The latter is the smaller and prettier of the two with many thatched cottages, and is fortunate to lie across the river from the railway, but both depend largely for their charm on their setting in surroundings of trees and flowing water.

Beyond the bridge at the west end of Stockbridge the Salisbury road rises sharply on to the high ground which carries on, with a narrow break for the Wallop Brook, over the county boundary into Wiltshire. The landscape is open and rather bleak, and there seems already a presage of the bare uplands of Salisbury Plain ten miles away to the west. It is a country well suited to the training stables and gallops of which there are several in the locality; of these Chattis Hill is perhaps the best known. There was once a racecourse lying a mile to the north of the A 30, but since 1898 it has not been used for public racing.

Just north of the old racecourse rises Danebury Hill, on the summit of which is a well-preserved example of a hill fort with a triple line of ramparts and ditches enclosing an oval area of 13 acres. The whole of the surrounding country is an open plateau, and from it the circular mound of Danebury Hill with scrub-covered flanks and crown of beech trees rises to a further 150 feet or so, and thus forms a dramatic incident in the wide landscape. It is easily approached from the east side, and a car park on the flank of the hill has been cleverly contrived with surrounding banks so as to interfere as little as possible with the beauty of the scene. The circular ditches and banks are important examples of Middle or Late Bronze Age earthworks, and must date from about 1000 BC. The outer banks, which have partially disappeared, enclosed an area of 38 acres, but the inner circle surrounding about 24 acres is still clearly visible. At a later date the innermost area was converted into a strongpoint by the creation of deeper ditches and correspondingly higher banks, which should have made the fort almost impregnable until the arrival of the Romans. Although the elevation is not very great there is a wide view in all directions over the rather austere open country of the neighbourhood.

To the west the plateau drops sharply down to the valley of the Wallop Brook, and in this valley lie the three villages which take their name from the stream—Nether, Middle, and Over. Middle Wallop is little more than a collection of cottages strung along the road which accompanies the stream through the valley, but the other two are very definite entities, and of these Nether is extremely attractive and possesses an interesting church. The cottages and small houses mostly crowd in the valley close to the stream and road, but the church stands boldly on the steep hillside south of the village. It can be clearly seen owing to its position, but is less simple to reach, as the narrow road which mounts the slope is not easy to find. However, it well repays the search.

The handsome flint tower at the west end dates from 1704, and in front of it stands an unexpected monument for a country churchyard in the shape of a large stone pyramid erected to the memory of a member of the Douce family in 1760. The Norman doorway beneath the porch, reset in its present position, is fine, but it is the size of the interior which is startling. The north aisle is almost as wide as the nave, and the length is also unusual, for there is a crossing where stout half pillars support Transitional arches opening into a very long chancel. At some time in the very complex history of the church a tower no doubt rose above the arches of the crossing, and this was replaced by the existing tower at the west end.

The arcades of the nave date from the thirteenth century, but the side aisles were enlarged during the two following centuries, and in 1845 the chancel was rebuilt, presumably on the original lines. An added embellishment to the church are the murals, of which that in one of the spandrels of the north arcade representing St George and the Dragon is the best-preserved—or perhaps the one most fully restored by the zeal of Professor Tristram.

Over Wallop has nothing of this interest to show—indeed the nineteenth-century church is rather uncomfortably intrusive—but the village is pleasant enough. The high open country to the north of the Wallops is a rather desolate agricultural area of wide arable fields. It must have been singularly underpopulated until the railway came and haphazard building grew up round the little station of Grately. The village is a mile away to the west, and this also is now fast expanding, but on orderly lines.

North of the village the Roman road from Silchester to Sarum, Port Way, streaks across the country, and parts of it are still in use as a minor road. To reach Quarley to the north the highway follows it for a couple of hundred yards or so, and then abandons it and leaves it to continue as a wide grass track until it is picked up again as a road a mile away to the north-east. The village of Quarley is not expanding, and indeed would call for no mention except for its curious little church. This stands agreeably, if a little bleakly, near the road, with meadows surrounding it on three sides. On approaching, one is immediately struck by a highly sophisticated piece of architecture in the form of a Venetian east window which seems a strange adjunct to the simple, barn-like little structure. On the exterior is carved 'Gulielmus Benson and Henricus Hoare F. A. D. 1723'. Professor Pevsner and David Lloyd point out in their invaluable Penguin of the county that this must be one of the earliest windows of the sort built in England, for William Benson was the first of the Palladian school of architects to revive the style of Inigo Jones and John Webb of the previous century.

The structure, to which this window has been so surprisingly added, is very ancient, probably Saxon or perhaps early Norman, narrow but high; the chancel arch is a nineteenth-century 'improvement'. Probably at the same time, the weather-boarded bell turret at the west end, a typical feature of early Hampshire churches, was removed, and the bells are now hung beneath a low, wooden canopy on the north side of the church.

To the north of Quarley the Services are very patently in charge of this corner of Hampshire; the Royal Air Force is at Amport and its neighbourhood, and the Army at Tidworth which lies on the boundary, with South Tidworth in Hampshire and North in Wiltshire. As a diversion, the former airfield at Thruxton has lately been converted to motor racing, and is said to provide a promising circuit. This presumably presents a new hazard for the local inhabitants, who having become used to the sound of aeroplanes will now have their summer days made deafening by the noise of racing cars. Thus, except for motor-racing enthusiasts, this is not a very rewarding area to explore, so we will turn to the gentle civilian country lying south-west of Andover.

Abbott's Ann is a spreading village with its church fairly centrally placed. It makes an interesting contrast to the usual run of parish churches in that it is built in brick with stone pilasters and was erected in 1716 by Governor Thomas (Diamond) Pitt, who owned the surrounding estate. It remained in the possession of the Pitt family until 1763 when the great-grandson of the 'Governor', who was a nephew of the great Lord Chatham, sold the property.

Thomas Pitt was an East India merchant and became Governor of Madras. The soubriquet of 'Diamond' arose from his fortunate purchase in 1701 of a vast diamond of 410 carats for which, after much hard bargaining, he paid the sum of £20,400. His dealings in diamonds had clearly already made him a rich man. The diamond was sent to London for cutting, where it was reduced to 136¾ carats, the cleavage and dust being valued at nearly £7,000. After long negotiations Thomas Pitt sold his diamond to John Law, the enterprising Scotsman who became Comptroller-General of Finances to the Regent of France, Philippe d'Orléans, and whose schemes incidentally threw the whole financial structure of France into chaos. The price paid by Law, on behalf of the Regent, was £135,000. The diamond was eventually placed in the French crown and was one of the few Crown jewels to remain unsold at the Revolution.

On returning to England with a large fortune the 'Governor' bought several estates in the southern counties including Abbott's Ann, and perhaps the building of churches—he also added a tower to the church at Stratford-sub-Castle near Old Sarum—may have eased any twinges of conscience he had about sharp dealings in the past. His church at Abbott's Ann is attractive, but was a fairly modest sop, and probably looked better before the Gothic tracery was set into the round-topped windows. Much of the original woodwork survives, and is simple and good.

There is a tradition in the parish that when a maiden or unmarried man dies, a chaplet is hung in the church, and there high on the walls of the nave hang these emblems of purity in two dusty rows.

South of Andover in the meadows bordering the lower reach of the little river Anton are the two villages of Clatford, Upper and Goodworth, the latter also bearing the alternative and less high-sounding name of Lower or Nether. Upper Clatford groups pleasantly along a bank of rising ground on the edge of the valley above the church, which lies low in the depths of the water meadows. It is a simple little building of many dates from the twelfth to the seventeenth century, not impressive in its exterior, but containing a peculiar feature within, a dual chancel arch—that is to say, a pair of late twelfth-century, round-headed arches in place of the usual single span. These arches appear to have been reset to span the chancel opening from their original position as a nave arcade; it was probably an economical, if inconvenient, arrangement devised in the late eighteenth century.

In the same parish is Bury Hill, a site of great archaeological interest. The hill, surmounted by three lines of banks and ditches, rises a little way to the south-east of the A 343, and shows three different periods of defensive works from the third century BC to the latter part of the first century BC, while excavations have shown that it was occupied well into the following century. The massive earthworks remain formidable and imposing.

Bury Hill is no more than a mile from the centre of Andover, one of those Hampshire towns in course of the painful process of expansion—from a modest population of 16,000 to one three times that size. Until lately it was no more than a jovial, busy market town sometimes almost throttled by the vast amount of traffic which passed through it (for it is a junction of many roads). Replanning of the centre and a by-pass road are an integral part of the new development. Architecturally there is not much of consequence in the town. The early nineteenth-century Town Hall in Grecian style, standing at the north end of the wide High Street, is a handsome building, and will perhaps eventually face a street less congested with cars. At the time of writing, however, it is a place better avoided. Broad new roads and round-abouts are extending outwards, particularly in an eastward direction, and the open farmland is fast disappearing beneath factories and housing estates. Scenically the loss is not very great, and the destruction of agricultural land is presumably unavoidable, but it is impossible not to regret the extinction of the pastoral character of the area.

The site of Andover was no doubt already an inhabited place when the Romans built their roads, but as always the roads were designed to connect major Roman towns and took no account of existing

18 Hale Park: the Forecourt

settlements. Thus Andover lies curiously in an angle formed by the Port Way and the road from Winchester to Cirencester, which cross at right angles a mile north of the town. A stretch of the Port Way towards St Mary Bourne has now been converted into one of the brave new highways, and the latter is still in use in a minor manner.

Further north, beyond the recuperative village of Enham Alamein, the area of High Hampshire begins in earnest. This is the mass of chalk country which stretches from a few miles west of Basingstoke far away into Wiltshire and covers large sections of the three counties of Hampshire, Wiltshire and Berkshire, which join at Rockmoor Down north of Linkenholt. With thoughts of the busy, highly-populated area in the south of Hampshire, it is difficult to believe that the almost wild, agreeably deserted area in the north-west corner is in the same county. The average height of the plateau above sea level is about 600 feet, rising, where downs take charge, to more than 200 feet higher, and dropping to a low level in the gently curving valley formed by the Bourne rivulet, to give this occasional stream its official name.

In spite of its sporadic character, the rivulet has provided names for three small villages along its course: these, from south to north, are Hurstbourne Priors, St Mary Bourne, and Hurstbourne Tarrant. The first of these consists of a collection of rosy-brick cottages, looking on to the magnificent trees of Hurstbourne Park.

The church stands charmingly at the end of a short avenue of lime trees leading down towards the Bourne. The tower in yellow brick dates from 1870 but the west doorway is twelfth-century somewhat rechiselled. There is also another fine arch of this period, probably once the chancel arch, now opening into a north chapel. Between the chapel and the chancel is a large open altar tomb to Sir Robert Oxenbridge, who died in 1574. The figures of Sir Robert and his wife lie on the tomb with representations of their numerous brood kneeling on the sides of the monument. Those holding skulls, about half the number, were presumably those who died young. The whole is surmounted by a rather clumsy classical canopy. It is in many ways typical of country monuments of that age, when flamboyance rather than fine workmanship was the aim. The overenthusiastic

19 *Romsey Abbey: in the north transept*

repainting has added to the former characteristic.

The Bourne may be no more than a rivulet, but the valley through which it flows is wide and attractive with many willows in the meadows. At one point a high brick viaduct carrying the railway crosses from side to side and adds interest to the scene with glimpses of green meadows seen through the tall arches.

St Mary Bourne spreads along both sides of the rivulet exactly at the point where it is crossed by Port Way, and in places the thatched and timbered cottages crowd close to the road. The church, on the east side of the road and of the stream, is large for so small a village, and not only large but also exceedingly complex from the architectural angle, with alterations and additions made in each century from the twelfth to the fifteenth—sometimes apparently twice in a century—while the south porch and the top section of the tower were early seventeenth-century embellishments, and the north wall appears to have been rebuilt later still. If one abandons the puzzle and looks at the interior as a whole, it can be said the many periods mingle into an attractive whole, while the rectangular shafts of the nave arcades with their corner columnettes are both robust and elegant. On no account should one be too bewildered to look at the font at the west end of the nave. It is one of the four in the county of the twelfth-century fonts carved in Tournai marble. This is perhaps the least important of the four, although it is claimed to be the largest, as its base is modern, but nevertheless it is a far from negligible feature of a village church.

The third village on the rivulet, Hurstbourne Tarrant, is the place constantly mentioned by William Cobbett, who preferred to call it by the name he considered the proper one, Up Husband. But, whatever may have been correct in the early nineteenth century, the former name has won the day. Cobbett had a great affection for the village, visiting it no less than six times in a single year, and it is sad that the thatched house in which he stayed was demolished some years ago. This is his description of the place:

> The houses of the village are, in great part, scattered about, and are amongst very lofty and fine trees; and from many points round

about, from the hilly fields, now covered with the young wheat, or with scarcely less beautiful sainfoin, the village is a sight worth going many miles to see.

The appearance is perhaps a little less Arcadian now than it was nearly a century and a half ago, but the situation in the deep valley with hills rising to the south and north is exceedingly picturesque, while the adjacent rolling country of wide, open landscape interspersed with areas of woodland has charm and a rather austere beauty. The church of Hurstbourne Tarrant, long and low with a bell-tower topped with a short shingled spire, has an undistinguished exterior, but is unexpectedly handsome within, although as usual the nineteenth century has laid its severe hand on it. But the nave arcades of the thirteenth century supported on circular columns are noble on a modest scale.

In Cobbett's day, that is to say in the early 1820s, there was no overall level of farmworkers' wages, and he was horrified to discover that at Up Husband, where the land grew admirable crops, a labourer was paid no more than six shillings a week, so that many of the families were on the brink of starvation. In other parts of the country the average wage was nine shillings but even with what they could raise on their own holdings the condition of the peasant families must have been appalling, and there was real cause for Cobbett's indignation. His words were none too strong:

> What injustice, what a hellish system it must be, to make those who raise it [the food], skin and bone and nakedness, while the food and drink and wool are almost all carried away to be heaped on the fund-holders, pensioners, soldiers, dead-weight and other swarms of tax-eaters.

As on other occasions Cobbett in his justified fury weakened his case by attacking those against whom he bore a grudge.

Two roads cross in the narrow street of the village: the A 343 from Andover descends steeply from a height of over 600 feet into the valley and rises on the far side to continue to Newbury; and a smaller road winds in a north-westerly direction up the valley and so into the high country which fills this remote corner of the county. It is an area I recommend highly to those who like driving along pretty lanes through a very sparsely inhabited and entirely unspoilt countryside. There are, too, some attractive little hamlets such as Ibthorpe and Upton, both true hamlets, as neither has a church, but containing a number of flint and brick cottages with thatched roofs, and also several small eighteenth-century houses built in brick for small gentry or for prosperous farmers. In fact these trim, comfortable houses, often attended by spreading farm buildings, suggest that farming in this region was a profitable pursuit in the eighteenth century, as it still is.

In the Middle Ages, however, I think, the situation must have been different, for the churches are extremely small and give no indication of wealth at this early period, and some are strangely placed. The church of Vernham Dean, for example, is at least a mile away from the charming collection of cottages and little houses which forms the village, and is perhaps not worth seeking out for it is a simple flint structure mostly of the nineteenth century, though the handsome west doorway is early thirteenth, but its setting is attractive.

The lanes seldom seem to connect the hamlets directly and prefer to wander apparently aimlessly about, their courses no doubt being dictated by the contours of the uplands, but it is rewarding to find one's way through Linkenholt, which is little more than a collection of large farm buildings, to view the prospect which is displayed to the north of it. The landscape here assumes an unexpected scale of grandeur. From this elevation of over 700 feet the ground falls in a wide, rolling valley of cornland interspersed with sweeps of woodland and rises to the smooth grass rotundities of Combe Hill and Inkpen Beacon beyond the county boundary. There are more romantic views, but the grand and simple lines here are impressive.

From these delights it is worth following winding lanes to Ashmansworth, a few miles to the east, where the little church to the south of this scattered village is distinctly out of the ordinary. The greater part of the church is twelfth-century, the nave early and the chancel late, and these are connected by one of the smallest chancel arches I have seen in any church, little larger than a doorway. On either side squints have been cut through the walls to allow those at the side of the nave a glimpse of the altar. The east end of the church was rebuilt in red brick with the date, 1745, clearly indicated in blue headers. Round the chancel arch are frescoes, but their subject can no longer be clearly distinguished. A curious feature is two little galleries on either side of the west window, the one to the south being labelled in eighteenth-century lettering 'Earl of Portsmouth'. The stair has now disappeared, so that now the only access for his Lordship would be a somewhat undignified one by ladder.

Little more than a mile to the east beyond the Newbury highway in a direct line, but considerably more by the meandering lanes, is the small collection of cottages and farm buildings known as Crux Easton. Nothing could be less distinguished except for two features which excite interest: a minute eighteenth-century church and a fine avenue of lime trees leading to nothing. The former, a plain brick structure standing sadly in an unkempt churchyard by the side of a muddy lane, replaced an earlier building in 1775. A note of distinction, however, is provided by the semi-elliptical apse containing the altar, with its marble floor designed with a radiating pattern and lined with handsome pilastered panelling. The font, too, is of the period, and consists of a marble bowl set on a carved stone pedestal. This all adds up to very little, but it has a pathetic charm.

The avenue, it would seem, once led to the now-vanished manor house, in the grounds of which the nine daughters of Thomas Lisle created a remarkable grotto. This earned a laudatory verse from Alexander Pope, who often visited Lisle, and although the grotto has long since disappeared, the verse survives:

Here, shunning idleness at once and praise,
This radiant pile nine rural sisters raise—
The glittering emblem of each spotless dame,
Pure as her soul and shining as her fame—
Beauty which nature can only impart,
And such a polish as disgraces art;

But fate dispos'd them in this humble sort,
And held in deserts what could charm a court.

From these elevations, intellectual and physical, (Crux Easton stands 700 feet above sea level), we will descend southward towards the Test which runs in a wide shallow valley from east to west from its source near Quidhampton. The villages of Dean and Church Oakley call for no particular mention, but further south where the chalk hills rise once again is Steventon which indeed calls for mention, for it was here that Jane Austen was born in 1775, the youngest of the seven children of the rector, the Reverend George Austen. Here she lived for the first 25 years of her life and wrote soon after she was 20 the first drafts of *Pride and Prejudice, Sense and Sensibility*, and *Northanger Abbey*, though the books were not finally published until she had gone to live at Chewton in 1809.

Steventon was always a parish rather than a village, for there can never have been more than a few cottages sparsely scattered along the lanes which wind amongst the shallow slopes; but the Manor House, Rectory and Church must have formed a centre of life and activity. Now even this slight community is no more, for the Rectory was demolished more than a century ago, and the Manor House, a large spreading building, mostly nineteenth-century but with one long wing which appears to be Elizabethan, stands grim and derelict, sunk in a tangled wilderness which was once an elaborate garden with walls, pools, hedges and gravel drives. Thus, of this neighbourly trinity only the church remains alive, and this, it must be owned, is a sad little building which seems conscious of having largely lost its purpose. It still has charm, however, and some distinction. The plastered west end with a squat tower surmounted by a short steeple with the fronds of a vast yew tree breaking the rigid lines is attractive. Much of the structure is thirteenth-century, but it is naturally the memorials to the Austen family which claim the chief attention. A brass tablet was erected to Jane's memory in 1936, and there is a very pretty monument to Anne Austen, the first wife of Jane's brother James, who died in 1795, and a more formidable Gothic one to James, who died in 1819. A tragic tablet records the death of the three children of the Reverend William Knight, Jane's nephew, who were 'cut off' by scarlet fever within a few weeks of each other. Of archaeological interest is the Saxon cross-shaft standing near the pulpit, and thought to date from the ninth century.

To return to the upper waters of the Test, there are two little towns astride the highway which runs along the valley: Overton and Whitchurch. In neither is there anything to delay a motorist—except the traffic in the latter which can be highly thwarting at the busy crossroads in the town—but the road between these two places is decidedly attractive, as it passes along the edge of Laverstoke Park with a view across the river to the classical house in the further slope of the valley. Here, too, are the mills where paper for banknotes has been made ever since Henri Portal started the industry in 1712.

A mile south of Whitchurch on the southern bank of the Test is the minute village of Tufton, which contains an interesting little church in which much of the original Norman work is somewhat marred by nineteenth-century improvement, but, perhaps irrationally, a large eighteenth-century window seems entirely acceptable.

Further south on the other side of the river is the village of Longparish, where lived the Colonel Peter Hawker whose *Instructions to Young Sportsmen* is, I think, still read more than 150 years after it was first published. The colonel was a versatile writer, but I would suppose that his books on military subjects are now seldom consulted, while his *Instructions for Best Positions on Pianoforte* can be no more than a curiosity.

Longparish is well-named, for the scattered village stretches along the road to the adjacent hamlet of Middleton, where the parish church is to be found. The handsome, chequer, flint and stone tower was added in the sixteenth century to the existing thirteenth-century nave. The arcades on stout round pillars to the north and south aisles are handsome.

From Middleton a road strikes across the valley southward to Barton Stacey, crossing on its route a number of bridges over the several branches of the Test—some broad, some narrow—and providing a prospect along these gentle streams as they wind between willows and alders. Barton Stacey is not a particularly interesting village, but the church set in a churchyard, containing a number of large and ancient yew trees, has charm. The exterior was refaced in 1877, but the battlemented sixteenth-century tower at the west end is fine. The thirteenth-century arcades to the aisles have survived Victorian alterations, and the chapels formed by wooden screens at the east ends of the two aisles are unusual.

If, instead of going southward from Middleton, one turns northward, a small road winds pleasantly through woodlands known as Harewood Forest. It is not forest in the sense of the New Forest with ancient trees, but unlike some of the other so-called forests of Hampshire it survives as woodland with clearings of arable land. In part of the Harewood Forest, cheeringly known as Deadman's Plack Copse, there is said to be a monument erected in 1862 to the memory of Earl Athelwold, who was murdered on this spot in 963 by King Edgar—a Saxon counterpart to King David—in order to obtain possession of the Earl's wife Elfrida. I must in honesty confess that I have not located the memorial to this melancholy event, so I am not able to guide the reader to it.

This agreeable little road emerges on to the B 3400 only a short distance to the east of the alarming new expansion of Andover, so let us hastily turn back and continue down the sequestered valley of the Test to the pretty little village of Wherwell—pronounced, I believe, 'Horell'—where the timber-framed and thatched cottages crouch close to the road between a steep tree-covered slope on the north and the park of the Priory on the south. On this site, low in the watermeadows, there was once a famous convent founded by the mother of Ethelred, which flourished until the Suppression, when there was a scramble amongst Henry VIII's unscrupulous favourites for this desirable prize. The successful competitor was the ninth Lord De La Warr, who had prudently enlisted Thomas Cromwell's influence on his side. 'I beg your favour that I may obtain it before the surveyors of the same come to the King, for fear he should grant it to another.' Lord De La Warr was clearly a man likely to do well in the tough Tudor world.

20 *Mottisfont Abbey: the South Front*
21 *Mottisfont Abbey: the Drawing Room*

0 *Mottisfont Abbey: the South Front*

1 *Mottisfont Abbey: the Drawing Room*

CHAPTER FOUR

Over the hills

But not far away. On the principle of dividing Hampshire roughly into geological areas for the purpose of fairly compact description the north-eastern part of the county seems to form a convenient unit. A belt of clay country known as Reading Beds and London Clay interspersed with areas of Bagshot sands, extends in a long triangle between the chalk country which makes up the heart of the county and the boundary with Berkshire. It is the same geological formation as we shall find again in the south, as described in Chapter Six.

This triangle, then, has its base at Aldershot and Farnborough in the east, where sand is definitely to the fore and extends to a point at Highclere in the west, while Basingstoke and Odiham are the principal places on the southern verge. This change of soil from chalk to clay and sand creates a complete alteration in the landscape. In the place of high, open country with down-like hills, the country included in this triangle is generally low-lying and fairly flat. Where the clay comes to the surface oaks and elms are the predominant trees, and although the areas of woodland are not very great, there is much hedgerow timber. The landscape, indeed, is one we associate more with south Berkshire than with Hampshire. In the sandy areas to the east there are, of course, pine trees and heathland, the type of country which in Hampshire is almost synonymous with service establishments.

Since Winchester is the hub of Hampshire, I will assume that we are entering this north-west section from the south. The Roman road, now the A 33 to Basingstoke, would be the natural way of entry from this direction, but to get the full effect of the change of soil, and hence of landscape, on which I have been enlarging, I recommend the road up the Candover valley from Alresford, the B 3046. It is more interesting, more attractive, and above all much quieter. It brings one to the high point of the chalk country at

Farleigh Wallop, at a level of nearly 700 feet; from there the road descends steeply into the great plain which stretches away to the county boundary and beyond. The view from this point is vast, but it is its extent rather than its composition which makes it dramatic. Basingstoke, and its extensive activities, is two or three miles from the base of the slope. It is generally somewhat obscured by a becoming veil of mist, but otherwise the hedgerow timber and small woodlands provide cover for this rather highly populated area, and the countryside from this elevation appears little disturbed by the works of man.

Basingstoke, should one reach it, is a most unlovable town. It has never been remotely attractive, and at present in the uncomfortable process of expanding from a population of 25,000 to one more than three times that size, it is definitely unpleasant. The main expansion is taking place to the north, but in order to convert a small town into a large it is necessary to bring the centre into the right proportion. Perhaps when these great works are eventually completed, it will emerge as a fine and exciting modern town. It is an opportunity that one hopes will not be missed, but I would suggest that for the present we should keep to the by-pass which joins the London road on the east side of the town, and from there take the turning northward to the interesting village of Basing.

Until the coming of the railway this must have been a most peaceful little place, but now the main London trains roar past it on the north side on a level with the roof tops, providing, it must be owned, an agreeable view for the passengers, but greatly diminishing the tranquillity. However, railway lines by long standing have become more acceptable than new roads, and to the visitor who comes to see the two features of the place, the trains do not matter very much.

The two features are the church and Old Basing House. The former is a spacious building, constructed almost entirely in brick with some of the walls rendered. The tower over the crossing is in brick with stone quoins and is surmounted with battlements and stone pinnacles. The effect is distinctly noble. The interior, which is rectangular in plan with side aisles ending in large chapels, seems to me rather soulless; and this is, I think, due to the fact that the nave and piers to the arcades are painted in what appears to be an emulsion paint, with a somewhat prophylactic result. The greater part of the church dates from the sixteenth century, but the pair of arches to north and south under the crossing are Norman. An interesting feature is the altar tombs in the chancel, two on either side with a small doorway between the four-centred arches over them opening into the chapels. These are monuments to the Paulet family, though two have neither date nor inscription. One of these is to William Paulet, first Marquess of Winchester, who died in 1571. More informative is the charming wall monument by Flaxman to his descendant, the sixth and last Duke of Bolton, who died in 1794.

A few hundred yards south-west of the church is the site of Basing House, famous for the siege it underwent during the Civil War. It was captured in 1645, and an unexpected figure amongst those taken prisoner was Inigo Jones. The site seems to have been inhabited in Roman times, and further excavation is expected to reveal evidence of this period; but the great circular moat, which must have provided a formidable obstacle to the Roundheads, dates in the main from 1261. William Paulet, whose tomb in the church has just been mentioned, built a magnificent house within these earthworks, of a suitable splendour in which to entertain Queen Elizabeth in 1569. For nearly two and a half years the Cavaliers held out within their defences, but their numbers were reduced to 300 by the defection of 500 non-Roman Catholics.

On 8 October 1645 two breaches were eventually made in the walls by cannon shots, and the Roundheads, under the personal command of Oliver Cromwell, swarmed into the crumbling building. The garrison were taken prisoner, including Lord Winchester who was incarcerated in the Tower of London, but the four priests who were found were hanged by the ardent Protestants. A useful plunder worth, it was said, £200,000—a vast sum—was seized. The buildings, which were badly damaged, were demolished and the materials removed to other sites.

As a ruin Basing is not picturesque: it has none of the dramatic appearance of, for instance, Corfe Castle in Dorset, which suffered a similar fate. At Basing little except the outer gateway remains standing, and it needs a good deal of imagination to envisage from the scanty and partly subterranean ruins how the building can have looked in its prime. It is the great Plantagenet earthworks, with huge ditch and bank, which now impress by their scale, and the memory of the heroic defence which give drama to the site.

To reach the next place of importance, which is Odiham, one can avoid the main road, the busy A 30, and follow a charming minor road to the south of it. It passes through agreeably unspoilt country with a mass of woodland on the rising ground to the north. On either side of the road lie the two hamlets of Nately—Nately Scures, with a very small Norman church, to the north, and Up Nately to the south. The highway then winds through the pretty little village of Greywell, with a number of brick cottages and a church, again basically Norman, standing below the village in the meadows bordering a stream. On the north side of Greywell runs the moribund Basingstoke Canal, which once united that town with the Thames. At this point it disappeared into a tunnel, beneath the rising ground, which is nearly three quarters of a mile in length. The vast amount of money spent in the past on canals and railways no longer now used is a depressing reflection.

Odiham is undoubtedly one of the most attractive towns in Hampshire. It consists of little more than one wide and gently winding street, with barely a single ugly building to mar its beauty. The houses which present their bland façades to the street—some of these are quite large—date principally from the eighteenth and early nineteenth centuries, though several, such as the George Hotel, are much earlier in date. It would be difficult to find a more attractive array of pedimented doorways, fanlights, Venetian windows, and other pleasant and well-designed details of that happy epoch of building. The houses are admirably maintained, and many of the stucco fronts are painted in harmonious colours, but there is nothing self-conscious or 'arty' about the little town; it appears, as it should, a happy and genuine residential centre.

The church, which stands behind the south side of the main street, is not quite up to the high architectural standard of the domestic buildings. It is built in flint and stone and dates largely from the sixteenth century. The exterior is given character, however, by a handsome brick tower at the west end built in the seventeenth century. The spacious interior is rectangular in plan and this with the tower gives it some similarity to Old Basing church. A splendid modern window designed by Patrick Reyntiens has lately (1968) been erected at the east end.

A rather sobering note, in contrast to the prosperous-looking houses, is provided by the ruins of Odiham Castle. These are at the west end of the town, actually in the adjacent parish of North Warnborough, and close to the Basingstoke Canal. They consist of no more than the remains of the very early thirteenth-century keep, but the fact that this was octagonal, the only one in England, gives it archaeological interest. Its early history was fairly glamorous, for it was royal property. King John had taken refuge there when he was forced to agree to the acceptance of the Magna Carta. A happier memory is the establishment there of a royal stud in 1312 when the Sheriff of Southampton was ordered to find maintenance for 20 colts and seven grooms; and later a certain amount of domestic accommodation was added, but this has now all disappeared and only the mouldering flint and stone walls of the keep survive.

The road east from Odiham skirts the south side of Dogmersfield Park and is pleasantly timbered on either side. The house of Dogmersfield, which is not visible from the road, is a large, rather austere building erected in 1728 and not unsuited to its present purpose of a school. From the A 287 a small road leads southward to Crondall, a village not to be missed on account of its rather spectacular church.

The porch is approached at an oblique angle by a narrow avenue of lime trees, and the tall brick tower immediately strikes the eye. It rises, rather surprisingly, on the north side of the chancel, and was completed in 1659, having been copied from the tower of Battersea church in London. The reason for the unusual position was twofold. It was found that the original tower at the crossing was forcing the Norman walls of the church outward, so had to be demolished, while the tower raised on the north side successfully and ornamentally supported the walls at this dangerous point. The two little wooden balconies which connect the tower to the older part of the church are curious. The tall buttresses at the west end and on the south side were more conventional means of reinforcing the walls. Except for these seventeenth-century supports, the church is predominantly Norman, although there were inevitable nineteenth-century alterations. The stout pillars of the nave rising to round-headed arches are extremely impressive, and there is fine dog-tooth ornament on the Transitional arch to the chancel.

The village is large with several narrow streets, in which are a number of agreeable, if not outstanding, brick houses of the eighteenth century, enough at least to give an air of some distinction to the place.

We are here alarmingly close to the Service towns of Aldershot and Farnborough, and the unattractively spreading residential town of Fleet. I would suggest at once turning away from these places, were it not for one structure in Farnborough which is highly rewarding to visit, particularly for those who care to indulge in a little gentle melancholy: this is the mausoleum in which lie the bodies of Napoleon III, the Empress Eugénie, and their son the Prince Imperial.

It is not very easy to find, for no more than an inconspicuous drive leaves the London road on the north side of the town and mounts the hill to the curious conglomeration of buildings forming the Benedictine Abbey of St Michael. It is architecturally, if somewhat freely, modelled on the nineteenth-century Abbey of Solesmes, near Angers in France, and like its prototype remains uncompleted. The church, with the mausoleum in the crypt, which stands close to the Abbey, is a unit in itself. It was built at the expense of the Empress in 1887 from the designs of Destailleur, the architect of the flamboyant Renaissance structure of Waddesdon. To this mausoleum were brought in 1888 the bodies of Napoleon III and the Prince Imperial, where they lie in stupendous Aberdeen granite sarcophagi, presented by Queen Victoria. In 1920 the body of the aged Empress was placed in a third sarcophagus standing between those of her husband and son. Few places can render more sombre reflections on the fickleness of fate.

In 1881 the Empress had bought the house of Farnborough Hill, which stands in a park a little further eastward along the London road. The house was built in a romantic 'Tudory' style in 1860, and is now a convent school. The drawing-room is maintained so far as possible as it was during the Empress's lifetime.

Before turning away from this depressing area, there is one further nineteenth-century phenomenon which is worth inspecting, and this is Minley Manor, which lies between Farnborough and the A 30. It should be said at once that inspection is not altogether easy, for the house is now part of the Staff College and intruders are not particularly encouraged; but any enthusiast anxious to see this outstanding example of Victorian opulence and bravado can take the path to Minley church, a small flint building erected about 1870, and from this point can be seen standing on a wide terrace the crimson south façade of the house. The principal part of it was built from the designs of Henry Clutton between the years 1858 and 1860 and is constructed of brick with a lavish use of stone for the many ornamental details.

There was clearly a mid-Victorian enthusiasm for the early sixteenth-century architecture of France, for the French Gothic style with a touch of the Renaissance. Waddesdon Manor, for example, seems to have been inspired by the Château de Maintenon of about 1510, and the Holloway College is closely modelled on the Château de Chambord of 1519; Minley, however, has no exact precedent, and is a free rendering of the style of that period with a galaxy of towers, turrets, high copper roofs, elaborate dormer windows, tall chimneys and arcades. It subscribes to the Victorian ideal of balance without symmetry, and it must be admitted that there is definite grandeur in this ostentatious building, while its copious crimson brick outbuildings, the long avenue of Wellingtonias extending from the entrance front, and the formal gardens amongst which it stands make it an important monument of Victorian taste.

A mile or two from Minley, beyond the heathland on the north side of the A 30, is the village of Yateley, lying only just within the county boundary. It is a spreading, scattered place, no doubt pleasant to live in, but of little beauty or interest except for the church, which has several unusual features. It stands by the small green which forms the centre of the older part of the village, and one is immediately struck by the curious tower. The body of the church is rendered, but the tower at the west end has a timber-framed base with brick infilling and is as wide as the nave; it is surmounted by a shingled bell-turret and a low spire. The space within it is remarkable, with vast beams supporting the superstructure. It dates, like the porch, from 1450, and is a strange rather than a graceful edifice. The main body dates from many periods, with the principal emphasis on mid-fourteenth century, to which date belongs the arcade supported on octagonal pillars to the wide south aisle; but the nineteenth century was not backward in leaving its mark. On the south wall of the aisle is a formidable monument to Sir Richard Ryves, who died in 1671. It consists of a large white marble urn supported on a free-standing black and white marble pillar, the whole set in a tall grey marble niche. Like the tower, it is inelegant but full of character.

A few miles further west, and also on the county boundary, is the village of Eversley, which unexpectedly has its church, the chief feature of interest, a mile or more to the south of the principal collection of houses. It is an agreeable but simple brick building dating from 1724, with a tall battlemented tower in the same medium erected nine years later. The simple interior is whitewashed, but is given interest by several attractive monuments. Amongst them is one to the architect John James, of Greenwich, who died in 1746 and may well have designed the church. In the same year as the erection of the church, he built for himself Warbrook in the parish, an agreeable brick house facing a long canal. It is not, however, open to the public.

John James is perhaps of rather specialised interest: a resident more widely known was Charles Kingsley. He became curate of the parish in 1842, and two years later became rector and remained so until his death in 1875. The Rectory, in which he lived, is a pleasant, undistinguished house standing near the church, and here many of his books, including *The Water Babies*, were written. His grave, with that of his wife, is in the churchyard beneath the spreading branches of one of the largest Scots pines I have ever seen. On the base of the marble cross are engraved the words *Amavimus, Amamus, Amabimus*.

In the southern part of the parish of Eversley stands the finest, the most splendid, house in the whole of Hampshire. This is Bramshill. I would like to guide you down the straight drive from the gatehouse and up to the tremendous stone Jacobean frontispiece behind which stretches the symmetrical brick body of the house facing eastwards over the garden and the park. But Bramshill is now the Police College and not open to the public, so I fear that if I indulge in transports of enthusiasm, I shall only excite interest which cannot be satisfied; so I will confine myself to a few dates and details.

The house was built in the years following 1602 by Lord Zouche, who bought the estate in that year, and his works were sufficiently completed to entertain James I in 1620. In the following year the Archbishop of Canterbury came to Bramshill to consecrate the chapel. This visit was the occasion of a most unfortunate accident. The Archbishop, as a relief to his spiritual duties, went hunting in the park, and in the course of the hunt he shot and killed a gamekeeper. The outcry raised by the Puritan party at this distressing event compelled the King to suspend the Archbishop from all his duties. He was eventually restored to his position, but his reputation for piety was for ever tarnished.

The entrance frontispiece, recessed between projecting wings, is in its elaboration typical of the complex designs favoured in the Jacobean period, and no doubt represents the last phase of the building programme, but the east front, which is the other principal façade, with its long range of stone, mullioned windows looking on to a balustraded terrace and terminated at either end by two bay arcades in the projecting wings, is more attractive. Here is grace and restraint unusual at this time, and these are qualities repeated at the north end of the house which looks on to a walled garden.

The Bramshill property passed through several families until it was bought in 1700 by Sir John Cope, whose descendants owned it for more than two and a quarter centuries. I visited the house several times while it was still in their possession, and it had its complement of fine furnishings, tapestries and family pictures, furniture and mirrors. The place had an appearance of superb, if decaying magnificence, somewhat increased by tin baths in some of the rooms catching rainwater dripping through the ceilings. I visited it again when it had been taken over as the Police College. The structure was well-restored and well-maintained, but inevitably all atmosphere in the interior had departed. It has no more than the academic interest, for example, of a Romanesque cloister reerected in a museum. The exterior, however, still retains its serene beauty, and in one direction has even improved: the garden is now perfectly kept up. When I commented on this happy fact I was told that the work was done by parties from Winchester Gaol. What an enviable arrangement! The supply of prisoners never fails: it is far otherwise with gardeners.

A couple of miles south-west of Bramshill is a small house belonging to the National Trust, and so open to the public on Wednesdays and Bank Holidays. This is West Green House. It is a charming house built in brick and dating from the early eighteenth century with the attractive architectural feature of busts set in roundels decorating the garden front.

There is not very much in this area to charm the eye from the landscape angle, for the country is rather flat and unadventurous, although well provided with trees. The villages add little to the picturesqueness of the scene, but several contain churches which are worth visiting. Mattingley, on the Odiham–Reading road, for example, has a church which is unusual in being timber-framed with brick infilling. The nave and chancel date from about 1500, but the side aisles were added in 1867. Thus the moulded wooden pillars supporting the timbers of the roof are original on the nave side but nineteenth-century towards the aisles. It is altogether an instance of domestic construction being used for an ecclesiastical purpose. Timber, in this well-wooded country, was plentiful: stone, a more usual material for churches, was non-existent.

Another church in the close neighbourhood in which timber features largely is Hartley Wespall. The village is connected to Mattingley by one of the winding little roads which wander bafflingly about this area. This also was once a timber-framed structure, but drastic rebuilding in the late nineteenth century allows only the highly dramatic west end to show its original mid-fourteenth-century date. This end wall has diagonal struts of tremendous strength forming a diamond pattern crossed by another upright and with the interstices filled with plaster. In the gable end, above a beam at roof-plate level, is more timber decoration, but lighter in scale. This rather humble church contains a large marble monument to Abigail, Lady Stawell, who died in 1692. As a descendant of this lady, I feel glad she was commemorated with so much pomp and taste.

Hartley Wespall lies close to the vast park of 1,000 acres or so surrounding the house of Stratfield Saye. It forms the centre of the estate which was presented to the first Duke of Wellington by the nation in 1817 as a token of gratitude for the victory of Waterloo. The house, long and low and stuccoed over brick, dates from 1630, and the side wings with curving Dutch gables like the centre were heightened in 1847. It is not open to the public, but a glimpse of the entrance front can be seen from the interesting church which stands a few hundred yards away to the west. It was built in 1784 in the form of a Greek cross with a low octagonal drum covered with a flat dome at the crossing. It contains a number of monuments to the Pitt family, from whom the estate was purchased by the nation, and to the descendants of the first Duke of Wellington.

A rather provoking characteristic of this part of the country is the manner in which the small roads wander about the flat landscape. Almost it would seem, as a protest against the direct lines taken by the Roman roads, the lanes seem to be devised without objective but with great prodigality, so that those ignorant of the area are in a constant state of bewilderment as no road ever leads directly from one village to another, but instead makes an objectiveless excursion into the deeper country before deciding with much hesitation to reach a village which may be close by.

From Stratfield Saye, then, lanes lead westward in the discursive manner of the area to Silchester, a place famous for its Roman remains, but boasting also an agreeable church at which we will first glance. The village is widely scattered and uninteresting, and the church stands away to the east of the principal congregation of houses. It is curious in plan in that it is roughly square with a very long chancel but without an arch to mark the transition, but in place of it there is a finely carved wooden screen. There are slight remains of Norman walling in the nave, but the greater part dates from the fourteenth century, while the chancel was built a century earlier. It is one of the rare churches which has not suffered from overenthusiastic nineteenth-century restoration, and so retains a mellowness which many churches of greater architectural importance have lost.

The church stands on the east side of the site of the Roman town. This was called Calleva Atrebatum, and was founded in a position already made into a defensive point by the Celts. Usually the Celtic earthworks were raised on bleak, open sites which were as unalluring to the Romans as places of habitation as they would be to ourselves, and thus they were seldom developed by the invaders; but Silchester was an exception. In this low-lying country the site is no more than slightly elevated, and the 300 feet to which it rises affords distant views to the south and east over a countryside which is still richly wooded. The first Roman town seems to have covered about 85 acres, but later in the first century AD this was expanded so that the earthworks enclosed an area of 235 acres and a grid plan of streets was laid out. In the third century the walls, which in part still exist, were built round the central part of the town. The walls were pierced by four main gates directed to the main points of the compass, and from these the long straight roads stretched away across the countryside—southwards to Winchester, south-west to Old Sarum, west to Cunetio (now Mildenhall) in the valley of the Kennet, east to London; only to the north was there no road, or at least no trace now survives, from this great junction of highways.

Although there is now little indication of the layout of the town visible within the walls, excavations carried on at the end of the last century have made the plan perfectly clear. In the very centre was the rectangular Forum surrounded by the typical grid of streets, of which the principals led to the gates. South of the Forum was a temple, with two others on the east side close to the present church, further east and outside the walls was the circular Amphitheatre.

Once the excavations had been complete and exact plans made the ground was once again returned to farm use, but three pavements were removed and are now set in the stone flagged floor of Stratfield Saye House.

It is not known when or why Silchester died as a city. In general towns of Roman foundation are thriving cities today. Winchester, for example, which was no more important, has never ceased to be inhabited although it has known many vicissitudes, while the reason for the abandonment of Old Sarum is well known; in 1220 it was decided to build a new cathedral on a more congenial site in the meadows bordering the Avon, thus the new town grew round it and the old town on the bleak and waterless hill top a mile or two away was deserted. But at Silchester the site had every advantage, and the excavations provided no clue to the puzzle. Perhaps it ceased to serve any useful purpose and decayed gradually, or perhaps some calamity befell it during the Dark Ages, such as a plague wiping out the population. It is an enigma which will probably never be solved.

Less than two miles south of Silchester, but perhaps a little further by the wandering roads, is the village of Bramley which possesses one of the most interesting churches of this area. A curious characteristic of these parts is that parish churches so often stand some way from the principal centres of habitation. This is the case to some degree at Bramley, where the chief congregation of houses is half a mile away near the station, but it is particularly noticeable at Silchester, at Pamber End, and perhaps even more so at Winchfield, some miles to the south-east, where the basically Norman little church stands pleasantly in the meadows at least half a mile away from its village.

The exterior of Bramley church is immediately attractive, with its curious mixture of periods and materials, brick, stucco, and flint. The sturdy tower at the west end is built in the first of these and dates from 1636, the porch and the south transept are in the same medium, while the domestic-looking area round the porch with a Tudor dormer window in the roof is stuccoed, and the chancel is flint. The interior is no disappointment and an immediate impact is made by the robust sixteenth-century pews, which have miraculously survived, and the graceful wooden gallery supported on fluted Ionic columns at the west end dating from the early eighteenth century. The south transept was designed in a thin Gothic manner by Sir John Soane in 1801. As architecture it is poor, but in its centre stands a splendid marble monument to Bernard Brocas, who died in 1777. His figure lies on a mattress supported by a weeping woman, while the ends of the marble base are finely carved with scenes emblematic of charity, justice, fortitude and other noble qualities which the deceased presumably possessed. The sculptor is unknown, but he may well have been Thomas Carter, whose rather similar monument to Chaloner Chute we shall be admiring at The Vyne very shortly.

But this is not all, for on the walls of nave and chancel a number of mural paintings have survived. One in the nave is a thirteenth-century representation of the murder of Thomas à Becket, one of the earliest known paintings of this scene, and although much restored is of rare interest. Other murals, such as the huge St Christopher opposite the south door, date from two centuries later.

South of Bramley is the third great house in this area, and one to which I am fortunately able to lead you since it is the property of the National Trust. This is The Vyne, one of the loveliest Tudor houses in the country. The small road from Bramley to Basingstoke passes near the house and the long rosy-brick façade of the south front can be seen across a stretch of park. The walls and the E-shaped form are due to Lord Sandys, who built the house between the years 1500 and 1520, but the stone window surrounds are mid-seventeenth-century and the wooden sashes eighteenth. The porch was added in 1654. The north front facing the lake is more impressive, for here the end projections rise to square towers three storeys in height, and the central block, which has a battlemented parapet, is dominated by a splendid portico added at the same period as the porch on the south side, and almost certainly designed by John Webb, the colleague and relative of Inigo Jones. Whether Webb was the architect or no, it is certainly the earliest classical portico on any English country house.

Since The Vyne was bequeathed to the Trust in 1956 by Sir

Charles Chute, whose predecessors had owned the property for three centuries, the interior has been carefully restored to an admirable condition without any loss of charm or atmosphere. There are many attractive rooms in the house containing some fine furniture and interesting pictures, and the Tapestry Room on the first floor gets its name from the panels of early eighteenth-century Soho tapestry with which it is lined. The *chinoiserie* scenes against a dark blue background have great beauty.

Perhaps the most notable rooms are the two long galleries in the west wing, the Stone Gallery on the ground floor and the Oak Gallery on the first. A number of large houses of the period have one gallery, few have two. The former is plain, and with its stone-flagged floor is practically a garden room, but the latter is far more elaborate. It is lined for its whole length from floor to ceiling with its original linenfold panelling, having badges carved at the top and bottom of each panel. It dates from about 1520, but the marble chimney-piece surmounted by a broken pediment dates from the middle of the seventeenth century.

There is much else of interest in the house. The dramatic classical staircase, designed by the owner of the house, John Chute, in about 1765, is an unexpected but altogether agreeable surprise within these Tudor walls, and the Chapel at the east end of the house contains its original sixteenth-century woodwork; and the stained glass in the Gothic windows is Flemish of the same period. In the adjoining Tomb Chamber is the monument already mentioned bearing the recumbent figure of the founder of the Chute family fortunes, Speaker Chaloner Chute, who died in 1659. The monument, however, was set up by his descendant, John Chute, in 1775, and was the work of Thomas Carter.

The Vyne is in the parish of Sherborne St John, the village lying in part on the line of the Roman road from Winchester to Silchester, while the remainder is scattered along a tangle of small roads. The church, concealed from the highway by a tall barrier of yew trees, has a curious appearance, with the fourteenth-century nave and chancel built in stone and flint in one without a break, while the spiky west tower surmounted by a green copper spire dates from

1837. The charming south porch in brick and stone with a four-centred entrance arch is conveniently dated 1533. The church contains several monuments of interest, of which the altar tomb standing in an opening between the chancel and the north chapel is the most important. On the monument lie the full-length figures of Ralph Perall and his wife, and the date, which is not mentioned, would appear to be about the same as the porch.

The adjoining village of Monk Sherborne contains an early Norman church, the walls of which are built of flint laid in herringbone fashion. It is not a spectacular building but interesting owing to its antiquity, and it stands charmingly on a rise with a churchyard sloping into the valley. The contrast between the rugged grey walls and the tile-hung bell turret is curious.

In the same parish are the remains of Monk Sherborne Priory, the thirteenth-century presbytery of which now forms the church for the hamlet of Pamber End. The Priory was founded in the twelfth century, and flourished until the Dissolution, when a large part of the stone of the structure was removed for other buildings. As a result of these depredations the transepts, chapels and nave have disappeared, and only the chancel and the crossing with the tower above it survive.

The Priory was once secluded in the midst of Pamber Forest, which covered much of this area, but which is now reduced to a few hundred acres of woodland astride the site of Port Way, the Roman road from Silchester to Old Sarum. The church and its ruins form a melancholy and lonely little group in this generally rather highly populated part of the county, and it is not easy to find as it lies off a by-road from the A 340 sharing an approach road to a farm down an avenue of oak trees. The interior is distinctly austere and unadorned, with four tall windows on either side and rugged oak pews designed for endurance rather than for comfort.

An extreme contrast to these sparse survivals of mediaeval building is the church at Wolverton three miles or so to the west. It stands in a corner of the park of Wolverton House a little way to the north of the A 339. It was built in 1717 in red brick with a liberal use of stone for quoins and other dressings. The tall three-stage tower

23 *The Vyne: the East Front*

24 *Kingsclere church*
25 *Wolverton church*

at the west end has a distinctly important air which is not quite achieved by the rest of the building. In the nineteenth century flimsy brick mullions were put into the window openings, with unfortunate effect. On the whole, however, the interior remains much as it was built, and is a good and rare example of a church built during the reign of the first George, which was a period when there was greater interest in building country houses than places of worship.

We have now reached the point of the triangle covered by this chapter, which is bordered by the chalk hills on the south side and the county boundary on the north. The principal places in this area are the three parishes with the termination of Clere to their names —Kings, Burgh, and High, to put them in the order in which we shall visit them.

Kingsclere, the largest of these villages, indeed almost a little town, just squeezes into the clay area, for it lies at the foot of the steep chalk downs which almost enfold it. It is a junction of many roads, those crossing the high ground on the south and east and those branching away towards the north and so into Berkshire. Along this small complex of roads there are a number of attractive houses of the eighteenth century and of later date. The church on the south side of the village is a spacious building, with a handsome tower at the crossing. The nave walls and the transepts are largely twelfth-century, and much of the chancel is thirteenth, but it must unfortunately be owned that the prevailing effect is of the nineteenth, when it was rigorously restored. It contains, however, in the south chapel, a splendid monument to Sir Henry Kingsmill, who died in 1625, and his wife. It is in black-and-white marble and the figures are carved in alabaster; it was erected by the widow in 1670. Sir Henry is portrayed in armour of Charles I's reign, while Lady Kingsmill is elaborately dressed in the fashions of a slightly later period.

Burghclere, a large parish four miles west of Kingsclere, is divided into two sections: Old Burghclere, a very sparse congregation of houses, and Burghclere proper two miles to the north. The church at the former is a sad, shabby structure set in a churchyard where even the paths, when I went there, were deep in grass. But it is an ancient

24 *Kingsclere church*
25 *Wolverton church*

building, the greater part of the long, rather featureless nave dating from soon after 1100, though the west end with a handsome Gothic doorway dates from a century later. From the south wall a mausoleum of the Carnarvon family projects into the sea of weeds and nettles, and adds to the air of neglect with crumbling walls and saplings growing through the roof. In the chancel a tiled plaque in brown and yellow commemorates those members of the family who are there buried, and a marble bust by Bartolini of Rome of the second Earl of Carnarvon stands forlornly on a window ledge. The churchyard abuts on to a wide arable valley beyond which the smooth outline of Beacon Hill rises to a height of over 850 feet. The summit of this majestic down is circled with the banks and ditches of an Iron Age fort, which must have been one of the most impregnable in the south of Britain. Within these earthworks is the grave of the fifth Earl of Carnarvon, the Egyptologist, who died in 1923.

At the other Burghclere—New Burghclere, though it does not use the appellation—the church is nineteenth-century, but to many the interest in the place will lie in the Sandham Memorial Chapel, which was built in memory of a soldier killed in the First World War. The whole of the interior is painted with scenes of Army life by Stanley Spencer, an artist much admired by many. But not, I fear, by me. I find his clumsy, moronic figures, so nearly true to life as they lumber about their lowly military tasks, distinctly distressing; but my opinion is not, I know, generally shared and I have no right to denigrate paintings which are accepted as a great artistic achievement.

We now come to the third of the 'Cleres', Highclere. This consists principally of the Castle and the park which surrounds it. The vast house was built from the designs of Sir Charles Barry in 1839-42 in a Renaissance style, and it seems to have been modelled on Wollaton, the flamboyant late-Elizabethan house near Nottingham. The park, which is of exceptional beauty, was laid out by Capability Brown about 1775. It was admired by Cobbett when he passed through it—which unfortunately cannot be done today—in the autumn of 1821, and he wrote of it: 'This is, according to my fancy, the prettiest park that I have ever seen. A great variety of hill and dell, a good deal of water.' On the west side of the park is a church built from the designs of Sir George Gilbert Scott in 1869. The interior is richly ornamented in the high Victorian taste, and contains several fine monuments from the previous church—the one to an Elizabethan Richard Kingsmill is particularly splendid—which have been rather uncomfortably accommodated in the nineteenth-century setting.

From a lane crossing the hills to the west of the park there is a distant view of the pinnacles and towers of the Castle rising, like some strange cathedral, amongst the curving crowns of the trees. It is perhaps at its most romantic from this distance, so let this be compensation for the fact that a closer view is not available to the public.

CHAPTER FIVE

Heathland and hops

It may sound a curious combination to unite heathland and hops into one chapter, for the first indicates some of the poorest soil in the county and the latter some of the richest. But there they are, these unexpected bedfellows, with often no more than a bolster of clay between them. The region where this strange geological formation is to be found is the long stretch of country lying between the chalkland on its west side and the county boundaries of Surrey and Sussex on the east side.

To understand the situation and to clarify the cause of the sensational contours which are found in this area and which are so unlike the rather placid landscape in the rest of the county, it is necessary to know a little about the geology. But as this is a subject which is tedious to many, I will offer no more than a simplified account—indeed, anything very technical would be beyond me.

Just east of the village of Bentley in the north of the area now under consideration a narrow belt of upper greensand, barely half a mile wide, creeps into the county from Surrey. It broadens out at Binsted into a pocket almost three miles across, then narrows again to little more than a mile at the Worldhams, and in this breadth continues southward through Selborne and Hawkley. Thence in a width of only half a mile it passes in a great sweep round Petersfield between the town and the majestic chalk bastion of Butser Hill, and so moves out of Hampshire into Sussex. Closely accompanying the upper greensand, which it may be noted is in fact neither green nor sand, is a belt of gault, a marl and a clay of unsurpassed heaviness, which William Cobbett likened to 'grey soap', but which in fact in its adhesive quality more closely resembles plasticine. This adjoins a wide area of lower greensand which also is not green but is certainly a sand of the poorest and most hungry variety.

Here are found the long line of steep hangers, in places like cliffs dropping to the sea. This sensational formation is said to be due to the gault descending in all sorts of waves and undulations through millions of years to the sandy country which extends away to the hills of Hindhead. It is in this parched area that are found the succession of heaths and commons such as Headley, Kingsley, Broxhead and Sleaford. Generally at the top of these cliffs, but also sometimes at lower levels where the upper greensand has followed the gault, are the hop gardens, as pretty and well-ordered a sight when the bines are in full growth as it is possible to see.

Hop gardens suggest country covered with oasthouses, and there are indeed a certain number in this area, but new methods of picking and drying hops need kilns of a different sort. No one would now erect a tile-clad extinguisher-shaped structure of the old days, but the modern form is a large rectangular building with a great space below for the huge intricate machinery to which the bines are brought from the gardens, and with the drying chambers above to which the hops are lifted when they have been separated from the stems and leaves. Like all forms of farming, hop-growing has become far less romantic and sun-bonnety than it was in the past.

We might enter the area which is covered by this chapter along the Farnham–Alton road, thus accompanying the belt of upper greensand which does not produce the steep slopes until it gets further south. At Bentley, the first village to be reached, the country is still level and calm with the river Wey, little more than a stream, winding through a shallow valley on its dilatory journey to join the Thames at Weybridge. The houses of the village, several of them attractive eighteenth-century buildings, are strung out along the north side of the highway facing across the valley to the Forest of Alice Holt. This great area of woodland, covering a couple of thousand acres or more, was originally Crown property and is now administered by the Forestry Commission, which uses the former Ranger's Lodge as a research station. Oak trees grow well in the clay soil, and in the seventeenth and eighteenth centuries the fine timber was used for ships of the Navy.

The church at Bentley stands on high ground away to the north of the village, and contains some thirteenth- and fourteenth-century work as well as a good deal of nineteenth. In a house at the west end of the village the late Lord Baden-Powell lived for many years.

South of Bentley, beyond the shallow valley of the Wey, is the village of Binsted, standing on high ground, marking the northern outpost of the long steep line of hangers which has already been mentioned. Away from all main roads, it lies at the junction of four narrow, twisting lanes. The rather devious little journey through these lanes is worthwhile for the sake of the charm of this area of rural and unspoilt country and for the unexpectedly interesting church one will find at the end of it. It stands very nobly at the highest point of the hill to which the lanes mount gently from the surrounding country, and commands a splendid prospect of wooded hills to the south and west, while the low stone and timber-framed cottages standing round the spacious churchyard give it added importance.

It is a many-gabled building with rendered walls and a robust stone tower at the west end surmounted by a short spire. The windows in the late twelfth-century walls are small, and in spite of a clerestory of little windows above the arcades of the nave the interior is very dark. It is these arcades, four Transitional arches on either side supported on short stout pillars, which are the most distinguished feature of the interior, while from the chancel dual arches open into chapels north and south making the church roughly—but unequally, for the chapels differ in shape and size—cruciform. It is too fine a church, and perhaps in too prosperous an area, to have escaped nineteenth-century restoration, and this was fairly drastic but it remains a village church of unusually high standard.

Taking the westward lane from Binsted, in a mile one is back on the trafficky highway to Alton which bottlenecks through the village of Holybourne. It is one of the two villages—the other is Chawton on the west side of Alton—which will return to their original quiet charm when the new by-pass is constructed, and it will be easy to understand why Mrs Gaskell, the Victorian novelist, decided to spend her later years in this tranquil village. She bought a house named The Lawn for £2,600, raised from her publishers as an advance on *Wives and Daughters*, and it was to be a surprise for her husband. But death stepped in, and on 12 November 1865, when she was visiting her new purchase, she died suddenly.

Holybourne is now almost joined to Alton by building along the highway, but although there has been much modern development on this side of the town, the long winding main street of Alton flanked by a number of warm-tinted Georgian houses still retains a pleasant character, and modern shop fronts amalgamate not disagreeably with their more dignified neighbours and show that this is no period piece but a thriving and active market town.

The place has a long history. The Pilgrims Way passed through it, and as far back as the thirteenth century it was a place of some importance owing to its mildly strategic position; and it had the honour, too, of being favourably mentioned by William Langland in *Piers Plowman*:

> *Ye, thorugh the pass of Aultone*
> *Poverte inyght pass*
> *Withouten peril of robbynge.*

The most interesting part of the town lies to the north of the main road, for here stands the handsome church well away from the turmoil of the centre of the town in an area of tranquillity. The greater part of the structure dates from the fifteenth century, but four robust early-Norman arches still support the tower. It was on the north side of this intersection that the present nave was built three centuries or so after the construction of the original church. On the north face of one of the pillars can be seen the remains of fifteenth-century frescoes said to represent Henry VI with St Cornelius and St Thomas of Canterbury. A better-preserved memento of the past is the bullet holes in the massive oak south door, made by the blunderbusses of the Parliamentary troops in 1643 during an attack on Royalists who had taken refuge in the church. I do not know the outcome of the engagement but it is unlikely to have been a happy one for the King's supporters.

An unusual feature for so comparatively small a town is a museum, which is housed in a far from prepossessing little square of Victorian public buildings in the main street. It is called after the family of Curtis, who were for more than a century prominent in the life of the town, and of which William Curtis, the compiler of the magnificent book, *Flora Londiniensis*, and other botanical volumes. was the most famous member. The museum specialises particularly in all aspects of Hampshire domestic life, farming and the countryside.

To those passing through Alton it is the nose rather than the eye which provides the clue to the prosperity of the town, for, as becomes a place in this hop-growing country, it is a centre of the brewing industry. Watney Mann have here a large establishment, and close by it Harp Lager is produced in a modern structure of steel and glass. Both these breweries lie on the opposite sides of the main street to the church.

Those who know their *Vanity Fair* will recall that Joseph Sedley, returning to England from India in 1817, landed at Southampton, and when he was sufficiently reposed began a leisurely drive to London. 'Having partaken of a copious breakfast at Southampton, he had so far rallied at Winchester as to think a glass of sherry necessary. At Alton he stepped out of the carriage at his servant's request, and imbibed some of the ale for which the place is famous.' Brewing at Alton is a long-standing tradition.

Leaving Alton the highway passes by The Butts, a charming triangular green surrounded by horsechestnuts through which can be seen a number of agreeable little houses and cottages facing this open space. Almost at once one is in the village of Chawton, a name well-known to readers of Jane Austen's novels. For here she made her home from 1809 to 1816 in the modest red-brick house standing at the corner where the Winchester road turns away from the road to Fareham. The village is picturesque, apart from the lustre cast by Jane's residence here, with many thatched cottages and attractive small houses, while a previous owner, descended from Jane's brother, planted many lime trees all about the village which scent the whole place when in flower.

It was after Jane settled at Chawton that the three novels she had written when at Steventon were published, and here she wrote *Mansfield Park*, *Emma*, and *Persuasion*. She was secretive about her work and did not wish outsiders to observe her industry. As her nephew described it: 'She was careful that her occupation should not be suspected by servants, or visitors, or any person beyond her own family party. She wrote upon small sheets of paper which could easily be put away, or covered with a piece of blotting paper.'

In 1794 Jane's brother Edward had inherited the Chawton estate, and also Godmersham in Kent, from a cousin and took the name of Knight. The picturesque Chawton House, in which he lived, is fully visible from the Fareham road with the straight drive descending to the nineteenth-century church and then ascending the further short slope to the front door. It dates from the sixteenth and seventeenth centuries and with its mullioned windows and stone-rimmed gables forms an attractive group.

Jane had ample opportunity for studying the country house life which formed the setting of all her novels, and this she observed and recorded minutely, but the settings in which her figures move always remain vague. It was personalities which claimed her attention, not the architecture of the houses in which they passed their lives. It is always left to the reader to fill in the details of the picture for himself. In *Pride and Prejudice*, for example, Pemberley House, Mr Darcy's home, was 'a large, handsome stone building, standing well on rising ground, and backed by a ridge of high woody hills', and 'the dining room . . . was a large well-proportioned room, handsomely fitted up'. It was clearly not an Elizabethan house that Jane had in mind, nor even a seventeenth-century structure, or it would have been dubbed 'old-fashioned'. No, I think, it was undoubtedly eighteenth-century and perhaps Jane saw it as resembling Stoneleigh, in Warwickshire, where she often visited her relations. With Lady Catherine de Burgh's house, Rosings, we are even more in the dark. All we are told is that the park had 'beauty and prospects' and that the hall had 'fine proportion and finished ornaments'.

With Northanger Abbey, however, she ventures a few architectural details. 'The whole building enclosed a large court; and two sides of the quadrangle, rich in Gothic ornament, stood forth for admiration.' And of the windows: 'To be sure the pointed arch was preserved—the form of them was Gothic—they might be even casements; but every pane was so large, so clear, so light.' The only definite picture with which we are provided is of the little house to which Mrs Dashwood and her daughters retired, Barton Cottage, in *Sense and Sensibility*. The exterior, it is true, remains a little hazy, but we know the planning and the layout of the rooms, and the perfectly feasible extensions which Mrs Dashwood contemplated, but never carried out.

This is a digression, and we must return to contemplation of the countryside; so let us follow the road which runs south-east from Chawton to Selborne and passes into the heart of the hop country. A little way to the north of this road and close to the edge of the steep hangers which have here developed to a dramatic height is the little village of East Worldham and the hamlets—they are barely even hamlets—of West Worldham and Hartley Mauditt.

The church of East Worldham dates basically from the first quarter of the twelfth century, but the nave was largely rebuilt in 1865 with the original materials. In the south wall of the nave is an early fourteenth-century tomb with the bust of a woman in a wimple. This is thought to represent the wife of the son of Geoffrey Chaucer, who was the heiress of the manor.

A narrow lane, in places sunk deep into the soft, shale-like rock, winds through the cluster of houses forming West Worldham to Hartley Mauditt, where the little church stands isolated in a meadow by the side of a large pond. Many centuries ago a village bordered the lane, and the outlines of foundations can be traced in a dry season, but at some unknown date and for some unknown reason all disappeared. The great house, however, which stood near the west end of the church was only demolished in the eighteenth century, and now the little building stands alone, the sole survivor of a once-active community. The nave is robust Norman work, and the semi-circular arch opens into a miniature chancel the walls of which seem weighed down by the handsome seventeenth-century monuments. The south doorway, dating from about 1200, is particularly splendid for so small a building.

There is rich arable land with many hop gardens all about this area, but the mildly undulating landscape is not exciting. However, if one follows the lane past the church, a lane which seems almost like a watercourse so deeply is it sunken, one arrives suddenly at the edge of the great escarpment which extends north and south across the county. The view from this point is positively sensational in its extent. At one's feet as the precipice melts into a more gentle slope are well-sheltered hop gardens, while beyond them and below them on the heavy clay of the Gault seam are great stretches of woodland. As the clay gives way to sand there appear the vast areas of heathland, in fact much marred by military activities, but these defects are kindly obscured by the blue haze of distance, and it appears as a sequestered Arcadia sweeping away to the majestic outline of the heights of Hindhead just beyond the county boundary.

These three little villages of the hanger country are obscure, but little more than a mile to the south—as the crow flies, that is to say, but a good deal more as the lanes wind—lies Selborne, a village whose name is known far and wide. It lies at a point where the Oakhanger stream, a minute rivulet, has worked a valley through the hills so that the steep, beech-covered slopes seem to rise in all directions. It is this position which gives the place its principal charm, for architecturally, with the exception of the church, it is not very distinguished. But it is the *Natural History and Antiquities of Selborne* by Gilbert White which brought fame to the village.

To energetic walkers a climb up the Hanger is infinitely rewarding, and not unduly difficult. There are several paths, but the Zigzag is the one well-known to readers of the *Natural History*. It mounts through the woods, with here and there an almost bird's-eye view of the village lying below. The path emerges on to an open area at the top of the Hanger, known as Selborne Common, now in the possession of the National Trust, which is maintained in a state of natural and attractive wildness.

Gilbert White was born in the Vicarage in 1720, and died at the house known as The Wakes in 1793. About ten years after his death the first collection of his notes and letters was published. Innumerable further and expanded editions have followed. His house on the west side of the village street is now kept as a museum, sharing honours with the Oates Memorial Library. The appearance of the building has been much altered by late nineteenth-century addition in what may be called the 'seaside style', but the view from the back of the house across a meadow to the steep leafy slopes of Selborne Hanger remains as Gilbert White looked on to it, and saw so much that was hidden to less observant eyes.

William Cobbett in his *Rural Ride* of 1822 mentions Gilbert White in rather patronising terms. The name of the village of Selborne, he wrote, 'put me in mind of a book which was once recommended to me, but which I never saw . . . written, I think, by a parson of the name of White, brother of Mr White, so long a Bookseller in Fleet Street'. This was correct: Gilbert's brother was indeed a publisher and bookseller, and it was largely due to him that the Selborne letters were gathered together and published in book form. Cobbett seems later to have read the book, for he mentions it occasionally but not with any particular enthusiasm, and one supposes he was more interested in his own writings than in those of anyone else. Now, nearly a century and a half later, I fancy the gentle naturalist is far more widely read than the Radical reformer.

Opposite The Wakes a little green, known as The Plestor, leads up to the spacious church. Before reaching the south door, one passes the famous yew tree, one of the largest in the country and a veteran of great but uncertain age. It was naturally described and measured by Gilbert White and at that time had a circumference of 23 feet; since it is still in good heart, it has probably by now expanded another foot or more. The church was drastically restored in the nineteenth century, but the short robust pillars of the nave are twelfth-century, and give distinction to the building. The painting over the altar of the Adoration of the Magi, flanked by St Andrew, St George, and donors is a Flemish work of about 1520, and was given to the church by Benjamin White in 1793. The artist is thought to be Jan Mostaert (1470-1555).

A mile and a half north-east of the village, and reached by a turning off Honey Lane, a steep and narrow road which leads down to Blackmoor, is the site of Selborne Priory. It was founded in this secluded and sheltered spot near the Oakhanger Stream by Peter des Roches, Bishop of Winchester, in 1232. Its early years were exceedingly prosperous, and with royal assistance from Henry III and others a large complex of buildings was erected. In the second half of the fourteenth century the conduct of the Priory had become regrettably lax, and William of Wykeham, who made an inspection in 1387, found a disquieting state of affairs. The monks apparently spent much more time hunting than on their religious observances, while their robes were by no means as austere and simple as they should have been, 'appearing like beaux with garments edged with costly furs, with fringed gloves and silken girdles trimmed with gold and silver'. Even more distressing were irregularities which necessitated a rule that all doors should be locked at night so that 'no suspected and disorderly females pass through their choir and cloister at night'.

Improvement, if any, in the behaviour of the monks was apparently only temporary, for in 1486 conditions were so unsatisfactory that Bishop Waynflete decided to dissolve the Priory, and the buildings, which were already in decay, were demolished. During the past few years much excavation has taken place on the site, and the layout of the Priory is now fairly clear. There was a cruciform church more than 200 feet in length, with a cloister on the north side, while the sites of the usual attendant buildings, Chapter House, Kitchens, Washing House, Rere Dorter, and so forth, have been established.

Just south of Selborne, and still in this hanger country, are two little villages with churches so strikingly differing that it is worth making the short journey through the twisting lanes and deep valleys to glance at them. These are Empshott and Hawkley. The former is no more than a hamlet, and the curious little church hidden behind giant Irish yews almost had the good fortune to escape the Victorian passion for restoration—almost but not quite, for some particularly brilliant Doulton tiles in the chancel show that it was not quite forgotten. The low turret at the west end is said to date from the reign of William and Mary, and is ingeniously designed with glazing on its west side to throw light into the nave, which even with this assistance is very dark. But the surprise of the interior is to find that it has an arcaded nave dating from the thirteenth century. At some time, perhaps at the period of the construction of the turret, the outer walls were demolished and rebuilt further inward so that the side aisles were reduced to a width of a foot or two. The effect is extremely curious.

At Hawkley, a pleasant, scattered village, the church is far different, for in 1861 the old church was entirely demolished—its antiquity can be guessed from the presence of three extremely ancient yews in the churchyard—and a new building erected on its site. It was designed in a rendering of the Norman style by Teulon, who had a prosperous practice in erecting vast country houses for the rich and the noble. It is built in Langrish stone, a close neighbour of the Selborne stone of which many of the houses in the village are constructed, and if the exterior with its graceless tower is formidable, the interior with its neo-Norman arcades is very successful.

We will now leave for a time this romantic hanger and hop country and explore the heathy land which lies between the hangers and the county boundary. The main road from Farnham to Petersfield passes through this area, and it is close to this road that the military establishments of Bordon and Whitehill have grown up. Since in this little book I attempt to be selective rather than exhaustive, and only to lead the reader to places that seem to me to have either charm or interest, I do not propose to try and find any beauty in Bordon. The hungry, sandy soil of this district is almost useless for agriculture and much of it not even well adapted to forestry, so the War Department are welcome to it. We will cross it to the high ground which fills the eastern bulge of the county, where there is a little more of interest to be found.

The most picturesque part of this hilly country is just over the county boundary at Hindhead, and the road leading up to it through the villages of Headley and Grayshott runs rather tamely through heathland and pine woods. There may once have been an attractive wildness here, but now it is far otherwise, and it is closely populated with many little houses tucked in amongst the trees. The whole of this area seems to have developed as a residential complex, both villages and countryside, since the last century. Possibly a lead was given by Alfred, Lord Tennyson, who built his house, Aldworth, on the slopes of Blackdown Hill just beyond the county boundary, in 1868. His purpose in coming to what was then a secluded area was to escape from the tourists who troubled him at Farringford in the Isle of Wight during the summer months. From this angle Aldworth was not altogether a success: it would be even less so in these days.

The only village in the neighbourhood which has any sense of antiquity is Bramshott, and the approach to it from Passfield, with memories of the Sidney Webbs, is attractive. The narrow road runs between high, fern-covered banks, and for some of its length accompanies the waters of a branch of the river Wey. The church stands well in the higher part of the village, and is a rather imposing cruciform building with a late nineteenth-century spire. The nave is of the same period, but the chancel and the transepts are thirteenth-century. The sturdy arches to the latter are original, but those between nave and chancel proclaim loudly their Victorian origin.

Bramshott is not a large village, but it is the mother, as it were, of Liphook, which spreads in an untidy manner along the Portsmouth road, and possesses no church of its own. Indeed it is a place which has grown purely on account of its position at a junction of roads, and to the presence, perhaps, of its one old building, the Royal Anchor Hotel.

To the west of Liphook Woolmer Forest extends away as far as the Farnham–Petersfield road and beyond, covering many hundreds of acres. Conifers are the only trees which grow here with any success, and over much of the forest the soil is too poor even for these rather melancholy trees, so that there is much open heathland. Just to the west of the main road is the village of Blackmoor, which has an interest for students of Victorian architecture. The village is largely the creation of the first Earl of Selborne, formed in the years following his purchase of the property in 1865.

The major work was the building of Blackmoor House on the site of the original farmhouse in 1872. Alfred Waterhouse, fresh from his triumph of designing Eaton Hall (now demolished) for the Marquess (later first Duke) of Westminster, provided designs not only for the house, which is of considerable size, but also for a good deal of the principal pieces of furniture. Unlike Eaton, which was wildly flamboyant, Blackmoor is rather pinched and crowded in its haphazard grouping, but it is a scholarly rendering of the Tudor style. With the growing interest in Victorian architecture, Blackmoor will no doubt eventually be looked on as a building of beauty: it has not quite reached that stage as yet.

The house was the major work, but not the first. The church at the north end of the village, also designed by Waterhouse, was consecrated in 1869. It is a large and imposing building with a tall west tower, and it can be seen at once that it is the work of a capable architect. But like many Victorian churches it is rather soulless. Perhaps increasing age will supply a soul. There are many other buildings in the village, a school, cottages and so forth all probably designed by Waterhouse, while the conifers which abound, particularly near the house, provide a setting which was a Victorian ideal.

One senses that much of this part of Hampshire, not only the low-lying sandy country but also the high chalkland which stretches away for many miles westward beyond the narrow band of upper greensand and the hangers, was a poor, perhaps almost derelict district in the early nineteenth century. So many of the villages with their Victorian churches, houses, and cottages seem to have sprung into life at that time, and clearly many who had made fortunes during that prosperous reign bought estates and infused much-needed money into a poverty-stricken countryside.

Blackmoor is one example of a new and conscientious landlord bringing prosperity to his estate: there is another only six miles or so to the west at East Tisted. Although the principle is the same, the effect is different, for East Tisted is on rolling chalkland where deciduous trees flourish and conifers are obvious aliens. House, church, and cottages were developed over two generations and were begun early in the century; they therefore display more variety in style than at Blackmoor, where most were built within a decade. Cobbett passed that way in August 1823 and spoke with approval of 'the owner of East Tisted, who has recently built a new house in the park, who has quite metamorphosed the village of Tisted, within these eight years, who has, indeed, really and truly improved the

26 Selborne from Hanger

whole country just round about here'. Praise from Cobbett was exceedingly rare, and there were probably few landowners at that time who merited it. In general the land was in a state of neglect and decay.

The 'new house' which Cobbett mentions is Rotherfield, which stands beautifully, high in its park on the west side of the road which runs through the valley, and overlooks the group of church, rectory and cottages which lie below. The house was a charming Gothic Revival building in 1823, but in the next generation it was altered into a more formidable example of the mid-nineteenth-century Gothic.

A couple of miles further south along the Fareham road at Basing was another example of mid-nineteenth-century wealth reviving what may have been a threadbare property. Here the fortune which allowed the buying of a large estate came from gin distilleries. The existing house was greatly enlarged in a formidable classical style, the park was extended and drives were thrown out to any main road within a mile or so, cottages and farm buildings were erected, and a handsome church designed by Sir Arthur Blornfield in 1876 was built in a commanding position at Privett of a suitable size to accommodate a large community, the tall spire of which can be seen for a long way around. It was irreverently nicknamed the Church of the Holy Spirit. But this whole complex was destined to last for only two generations. The house is now demolished, the park has returned to arable land, the estate has been broken up, and only the church remains intact, a grave embarrassment to the reduced population which is expected to support it. It is curious how nineteenth-century enterprises of this sort seem to have been more evanescent than those of the eighteenth. They provided a parallel to the number of great country houses which were erected in France during the latter half of the seventeenth century, and which fell into ruin almost before they were completed.

The high plateau to the east of the Alton–Fareham road is criss-crossed by several small lanes and one larger road, but it remains a thinly populated area with only here and there a hamlet or little village. Prior's Dean, for example, is certainly barely the former,

27 *Petersfield Pond*

for it consists of little more than a tall seventeenth-century brick manor house, and opposite it, across a lane, a little church, which is worth visiting, both for its charming setting in a fold of the hills and also for its tough twelfth-century architecture. Further south is Froxfield, definitely a small village, with its houses spread out round a green, and scattered along narrow lanes.

Between Prior's Dean and Froxfield runs the Petersfield road, which is one of the most sensational in Hampshire, a county in general little given to extremes. This road winds down Stoner Hill, part of the long escarpment we have met further north, and in many turns and twists descends from a height of 700 feet into the plain more than 400 feet lower. The steep slopes are covered with beech woods, and between the trunks one has a glimpse of houses lying far below with the roofs of Petersfield a mile or so away to the south-east.

As the precipitous slopes flatten out, the road passes the complex of buildings of Bedales School, the well-known coeducational establishment, which came to this site in 1900. The road then carries on into Petersfield, the principal town of this part of the county. It is an ancient market centre, having reached great prosperity under the Tudors through the development of its trade in cloth and leather, to which its position in the midst of an agricultural region was conducive. These trades have disappeared, but it still maintains a busy, prosperous air, and it is clearly a place where slightly 'arty' shops do good business.

The two most attractive features are the spacious market square, with the church filling the south side, and The Spain, which leads out of the south-west corner. The buildings round the square have suffered during the past few decades—a particular loss was an interesting seventeenth-century house on the west side—but the general appearance is extremely agreeable, and the fine eighteenth-century equestrian figure of William III in the centre greatly adds to its distinction. Money for the statue was bequeathed in 1750 by a former Member of Parliament for Petersfield who was an admirer of this 'Avenger of Liberty'.

The church on the north side of the market place is of great interest, in spite of the almost inevitable overenthusiastic nineteenth-century restoration. The nave is fine early Norman work dating from about 1100, while the north and south aisles were added about 70 years later. The chancel arch has splendid zigzag decoration, and the three tall, round-headed openings above it are good examples of Norman detail. Altogether it is a church not to be missed.

The Spain is a tranquil area where picturesque houses are grouped along a small road with wide grass verges giving much the appearance of houses round a small village green. It is said to have obtained its name from the Spanish merchants who came here for the wool trade. There are pleasant houses of many periods to be seen in the adjacent streets, particularly in the High Street which opens from the north-east corner, and also along the London–Portsmouth road which runs through the town to the east of the market place. On the east side of the town is Petersfield Pond, which deserves the name of lake, for it covers a large extent, and is surrounded by an outpost of the sandy, heathy country which we have observed at the base of the hangers further north. The change in conformation caused by the transition from upper greensand to chalk is well exemplified in this area, for to the north of the town the beech-clad hangers on the former soil rise in irregular breaks and folds to a height of over 700 feet, while to the south the smooth, bare downs of the latter, dominated by Butser Hill which rises a hundred feet higher than the hangers, form a long bastion across the landscape.

Butser Hill fascinated William Cobbett, who rode over it on his way from Botley to Liphook and wrote enthusiastically about it:

> This is as interesting a spot, I think, as the foot of man ever was placed upon. Here are two valleys, one to your right and the other to your left, very little less than half a mile down to the bottom of them, and much steeper than a tiled roof of a house.

He then expatiates on the distant views obtained in all directions. As a dutiful guide I felt I ought also to climb on to the down and add my reflections on the scene to those of Mr Cobbett. But having no horse like the latter, the operation was carried out on foot, and very strenuous it turned out to be.

I decided to follow a grass track which left the road near the hamlet of Ramsdean on the north side of the hills. It winds at first across the meadows and then rises into a wooded area; from this one emerges into a winding cleft in the downs, with strange bleak hills on either hand sparsely covered with turf which barely conceals the chalk of their formation. There was complete silence between these austere slopes, with no wind and no sun, for the bottom of the valley is early cast into shadow, and there was no life of birds or animals to break the stillness. One seemed here to be in a different world to the rest of Hampshire, where the landscape is in general mild, indeed rather cosy. My path, after winding almost on the level, suddenly rose precipitously up the side of the down, and Cobbett's description I felt was well-merited. Breathless and exhausted I eventually reached level ground at the top of the ridge and was out once again into wind and sunshine.

From this height there is, indeed, a vast view. Southward one looks across the wide area known as the Forest of Bere to the long ridge of the Portsdown Hills, and northward across another great valley to the beech-covered hangers of Stoner Hill. But I feel that in honesty I should own that I have seen more beautiful views obtained with less exertion. The prospect from Old Winchester Hill, which I will describe shortly, and that from the hills beyond the Meon valley seem to me better composed and more romantic. But I would be reluctant to deter any who have the energy from following in the footsteps of Cobbett and his nag. Only later did I discover that I had scaled the hills the hard way and that had I approached from the south a thoughtful County Council had provided a passable road and a car park on the summit so that the prospect can be enjoyed without the remotest exertion. Nevertheless I do not regret my romantic walk, and I recommend it to the active.

The river Meon rises in these chalk hills, and on the principle of guiding the reader gradually southward between the area covered by Chapter One and the county border, which since the neighbourhood of Liphook has been with Sussex, we will join the river valley. The Meon follows, on its smaller scale, a similar course to the Itchen, in that rising at the northern base of the chalk ridge it flows first north for a mile or so then turns westward for three miles before adopting its main course southward towards the Solent.

At the point where it changes direction from north to west it passes through East Meon, one of the most beautiful villages in Hampshire. Its great distinction is the splendid Norman church, the finest village church in the county. It is not only outstanding for its architecture but also for its site, for it stands on the lower slope of a sheer down which rises on the north side of the village and so dominates the houses on the lower level.

Soon after the Norman Conquest the manor was seized by William I, and it remained in the possession of the Crown till the middle of the twelfth century, when Henry II granted it to the Bishops of Winchester. No doubt this illustrious pedigree accounts for the ambitious scale of the church. The nave, transepts, and arches supporting the tower and spire date from about 1130, when East Meon was still royal property, the south aisle and south chapel date from the following century, and the chancel from the fifteenth. The four semi-circular arches supported on short half-pillars of the crossing are a particularly important feature, but the whole church is an unusually splendid survival of mediaeval architecture. At the west end of the south aisle is one of the four fonts in the county carved in the hard and shining Tournai marble, of which the one in Winchester Cathedral has already been described, and dates from the earliest building of the church.

Across the road from the church is the interesting Tudor building known as the Court House, for it was here that the courts-leet of the manor were held. It dates from the early fifteenth century and consists principally of a fine hall and several attendant rooms. Having fallen into disrepair, it was bought in the 1920s by the architect Morley Horder (known as Holy Murder to his less appreciative acquaintances), and fully repaired. He lived here till his death in 1944.

South of the church a road slopes gently down into the main part of the little village, where it is ambitiously known as High Street, and then turns east and west parallel with the Meon, here still no more than a narrow stream, which is spanned by several bridges to the houses on the north side. Amongst these is a particularly handsome early eighteenth-century house in brick with a deep cornice below the roof which stands with great dignity amidst its more 'cottagey' neighbours. Altogether the village retains to the full its natural and unselfconscious charm.

Three miles westward along the valley of the Meon is West Meon, a much larger village than its neighbour and without its extreme architectural distinction. But nevertheless it is attractive and contains a number of picturesque cottages and small houses. The main road, A 32, passes through it and winds down southward in a graceful curve and crosses the Meon which here passes into the watermeadows of the shallow valley. The church standing on high ground to the north-east of the village was built in the 1840s from the designs of Sir George Gilbert Scott, and is not very rewarding to visit. But cricketers may be interested to know that Thomas Lord, the original proprietor of Lord's Cricket Ground, who died in 1832, is buried in the churchyard.

The A 32 wanders pleasantly southward on the east side of the Meon till it reaches Warnford, where it crosses the river which then passes through Warnford Park. The house, which had charm if no great architectural distinction, was demolished more than a decade ago, while the follies which in the late eighteenth century decorated the scene—such as a hermitage containing the wax figure of an anchorite fixed in the act of reading an apologia for the Church of England—disappeared long ago.

But the park still contains two structures of interest: the ruins of a building known as King John's House, and the parish church. The former, amongst trees just to the east of the church, has principally archaeological appeal, since not much now survives. It dates from about 1230 and is roughly contemporary with the Great Hall of Winchester Castle. The principal remains are part of the walls of the hall and two rooms at its west end. One of the four columns which supported the roof still stands; of the other three only the bases survive, with some lengths of flint wall more than three feet thick. Any connection with King John seems mythical: the name is probably derived from the St John family, who were mediaeval owners.

The church, close to the ruins, is largely Norman, and a date can be fairly accurately assigned to it, for a contemporary inscription records that it was rebuilt by Adam de Port. He held Warnford from 1171 till his death in 1213, and it seems certain that he built the tower soon after he came into possession, and the nave towards the end of his life. The sturdy, rectangular tower with twin circular openings on each face beneath the parapet is fine Norman work; the interior contains two handsome early seventeenth-century monuments to members of the Neale family, the larger bears the full-length figures of Sir Thomas Neale and his two wives, with the figures of their children, once ten but now only nine, on the side of the tomb. It dates apparently from about 1640, although the clothes of the figures would suggest a rather earlier date.

The house stood a little to the north of the church, with its west windows looking on to the Meon as it flowed through the park. There is inevitably a feeling of melancholy about a place where a large house has stood for centuries and the owners had delighted in planting the park and, in this case, expanding the river into a long sheet of water. The park still survives, but its purpose no longer exists.

The main road continues southward along the wide valley, crossing and recrossing the Meon, which has by this stage developed from a stream into a respectable river. On either hand rise the chalk hills which to the west form a long ridge as far as the Itchen valley, while to the east the ridge stretches away past Butser Hill to form the South Downs of Sussex. From Warnford a passable lane leads up on to these heights and crosses Old Winchester Hill, one of the beauty spots of the district. From this elevation of nearly 700 feet there is a splendid view over half the county with the corresponding down of Beacon Hill rising beyond the meadows in the river valley.

The origin of the name of this windswept down is mysterious, for the City of Winchester is upwards of 12 miles away to the west, but it seems probable that this commanding site was an ancient British stronghold and that it was given the name *Venta,* indicating a river valley through the hills as at Winchester where the situation is somewhat similar. No more than part of the earthworks now survive to show that this was one of the chain of strongholds which stretched right across the county.

Beacon Hill on the west side of the valley is less dramatic but it is a pleasant drive to take the road up on to the ridge whence there are romantic views both north and south. From there one can take the narrow lane southward through an area of unpopulated country and so drop down again into the valley where four villages lie close together strung along the banks of the Meon. These are Exton, Corhampton, Meonstoke and Droxford, to list them from north to south—not in degree of importance, for the last is much the largest of the four.

Exton, lying away from the road on the west side of the river, calls for no particular comment, but Corhampton possesses a small Saxon church standing on a bank above the highway. The east wall facing the road has been rebuilt, but the church still retains much of the original work, such as the semi-circular chancel arch and the tall south doorway. The walls of the nave have bulged and swayed towards the south, but seem to be stabilised at this eccentric angle.

A few hundred yards away across the river stands the church of Meonstoke, its timber-topped tower rising picturesquely from the watermeadows. The main fabric dates from the thirteenth century with some fifteenth-century alterations, but in spite of its antiquity it is not of outstanding interest.

Rather more than a mile further south along the Meon valley road is the fourth village of the group, Droxford. The road descends rather steeply and narrowly into the valley on a level with the river, which flows a little to the east of the village, and rises again in a gentle curve up the further slope. To those heading for the coast on a summer weekend the place no doubt represents no more than a bottleneck, but those with leisure can observe the very pleasant houses and cottages which line the street. It must be owned, however, that it is an example of ribbon development from previous centuries, for the village has considerable length but little depth. At the lowest point the houses fall back on the east side and here beyond an open space are the three principal buildings, the seventeenth-century Manor House, the former Rectory, an early Georgian building almost hidden by trees, and beyond it the church charmingly sited on the edge of the watermeadows.

Much of the twelfth-century nave and chancel still survives, but at various later dates openings were made through the original walls when aisles and chapels were added. The former date from the end of the twelfth century, while the handsome battlemented tower in flint and stone was entirely built in 1599, the date being obligingly inscribed on a stone above the west door. The disused north doorway is a good example of Norman work.

This, I think, is the only occasion in this little guide, which is designed to lead the reader to pleasant or interesting sites and sights, that I feel called upon to mention a railway station. Droxford Station, on the now-disused Meon Valley Line, stands embowered in trees on the east slope of the valley above the river, and so a little way from the village. Architecturally it is no beauty, but historically it is interesting, for here on the sidings were gathered coaches used by the most important figures in the country during the anxious hours preceding D Day and the invasion of the French coast. Here they endured the 24-hour delay in the launching of the enterprise while awaiting an improvement in the weather. In its anonymity it was a well-chosen place.

The A 32 keeps to the west side of the valley for three miles or so south of Droxford, and halfway along this stretch there is a charming view of the handsome sixteenth-century tower of Soberton church, rising majestically on high ground beyond the river. There is a tradition, probably mythical, that funds for building the tower were subscribed by the butlers and dairymaids of the neighbourhood. It is not disclosed why cooks and housemaids were not included in this praiseworthy scheme.

George Anson, the famous eighteenth-century admiral, lived in Soberton, and when he was rewarded with a peerage in 1747 after a decisive victory over the French fleet off Cape Finisterre, he took the name of Viscount Anson of Soberton. The following year he married the heiress daughter of Lord Chancellor Hardwick and moved from the modest surroundings of this little Hampshire village to the palatial house of Moor Park in Hertfordshire, where he died in 1762.

We have here reached the point where the chalk subsoil which covers most of the heart of the county meets the clay area which extends to the Solent, and since that part of the county is covered by Chapter Six we will now turn eastward and examine the district which lies between the Meon valley and the county boundary. The only village of any size and antiquity in this rather empty area is Hambledon. It lies very pleasantly at a junction of several roads which reach it through valleys in the chalk hills, some of which are covered with beech woods, and it boasts three features of unusual interest: it has an important church; it is well-known as the 'Home of Hampshire Cricket'; and on the edge of the village there is one of the very few serious wine-growing vineyards, so far as I know, in Great Britain.

The church stands at the top of a short steep street which rises to the north from the road to Clanfield. The street itself is bordered by agreeable little houses and the church stands majestically above it looking out over the roofs of the village, and with a vast hollow yew tree sheltering its south side. A splendid fifteenth-century porch of generous size leads into the nave, which appears at first sight very complex, for the original twelfth-century nave was largely extended in the thirteenth, but leaving the Norman chancel arch in its original position, thus dividing the nave into two parts. A slight break in the roof-line is the only indication in the exterior of the extension.

The vineyard is on the same ridge as the church, but on the western edge of the village. The slope on which the vines are grown faces south and receives all possible sunshine, and it seems the vines appreciate the limey soil in which they grow. In the Middle Ages there appear to have been many vineyards in the southern counties, and one is inclined to suppose that the climate of England was more Continental at that time than nowadays.

Broadhalfpenny Down, which is regarded with veneration by keen cricketers, lies a mile or so north-east of the village. It was not here that cricket was first thought of, for a game of sorts with bat and ball has been played since the Middle Ages, but this remote down was the birthplace of first-class cricket, and the Hambledon

Club, which came into existence in 1750, at one time provided so strong a team that it was able to defeat an eleven from the whole of the rest of England. A granite column now commemorates the feats of this famous club, while the name of an adjacent pub, The Bat and Ball, helps to keep the memory green.

Between Hambledon and the London–Portsmouth road there are only two villages, Catherington and Clanfield. The former has a church which is largely twelfth-century, but was rather formidably restored in the nineteenth. Indeed, as one approaches it the appearance is strongly of the latter date and it comes as a surprise to find within it a fine arcaded nave with short stout pillars supporting semicircular arches. Against the east wall of the north chapel is a large altar tomb bearing the figures of Sir Nicholas Hyde, who died in 1631, and his wife, while their ten children are portrayed on the face of the monument. It appears to have been restored in the nineteenth century, and little loved since then. In a spandrel of the north nave arcade some rather faded wall-paintings have survived representing St Michael weighing souls. They are thought to date from the middle of the fourteenth century, but have been much repainted.

Clanfield is best forgotten. It is a little village at a crossroads which has grown into a bungalow town, and one feels that Portsmouth has already stretched out its hideous tentacles into the countryside, so let us hastily retrace our steps northward towards Petersfield and then take the little road eastward to Buriton.

This quiet little village lies at the point where the narrow strip of upper greensand turns eastward and continues over the county border, so that here once again we find hangers and hop gardens as in the Selborne area. The village has expanded considerably in the direction of the Portsmouth road which runs to the west of it, but the group of buildings which made up the original community—church, manor house, spacious rectory and cottages—is little altered. It is set on either side of a gently sloping green with a circular pond at its lowest point, and behind the village rise the high, beech-covered hangers which seem to enfold it in their wooded embrace.

In the eighteenth century the estate belonged to Edward Gibbon's father, and the historian spent many of his adolescent years in the manor house, which, with the church, stands on the east side above the green. He describes the place in his *Autobiography*:

> My father's residence in Hampshire, where I have passed many light and some heavy hours, was at Buriton. . . . An old mansion in a state of decay, had been converted into the fashion and convenience of a modern house; and if strangers had nothing to see, the inhabitants had little to desire. The spot was not happily chosen, at the end of the village and the bottom of the hill; but the aspect of the adjacent grounds was various and cheerful: the downs commanded a noble prospect, and the long hanging woods in sight of the house could not perhaps have been improved by art or expense.

Gibbon's description indicates the growth of the house. To a long, low range, probably of Elizabethan date, was added in the latter part of the eighteenth century a handsome, three-storeyed block facing east. In front of the house is a spacious court, once no doubt a farmyard, bounded by a stable building and an exceptionally noble barn. The early wing of the house and the barn, as well as many houses in the village, are built of Selborne stone with brick dressings. It is a stone found in the areas of upper greensand, and with its mellow, milky colouring is extremely attractive. Although rather soft when quarried, it hardens with exposure, and is clearly long-lasting.

The church has a picturesque exterior with a sturdy tower at the west end dating from 1714 after the destruction of the previous tower by fire; but it is the interior which is the most impressive, for the nave dates from the latter part of the twelfth century and the stout pillars and arches to the aisles are excellent small-scale examples of the period. The chancel dates from about a century later, and has suffered more than the nave from restoration. There are a number of monuments, of which that to Leonard Bilson, who died in 1695, is an admirable example of Stuart carving. It is sad it should be almost lost to view on the west wall of the vestry.

From Buriton a lane, narrow but perfectly passable for a car, climbs steeply southward up the hanger on to the chalk downs, which here rise to between 600 and 700 feet. Many of the slopes are now clothed with beech trees planted by the Forestry Commission about 30 years ago and known as the Queen Elizabeth Forest. Now, in spite of the thin, poor soil, they have grown to a respectable size. Through a valley in the hills runs the main London to Portsmouth railway, and amongst the woods on the high ground beyond it stands, in a fine position, Ditcham Park, a formidable house erected in 1888 to the designs of Sir Reginald Blomfield for my maternal grandfather. It is now, like many other examples of nineteenth-century opulence, a school.

The narrow lane winds down through folds in the hills to the village of Chalton. Although the busy Portsmouth road is little more than a mile away to the east and the railway is on the west, the whole of this area bordering Sussex seems as remote and tranquil as anywhere in the county. There are two buildings of charm in this tiny hamlet—the church and the Red Lion public house.

The church stands high amongst trees above the narrow roads which pass through the hamlet, and from its position the battlemented west tower, built in all manner of materials—flint, stone, brick—has quite an imposing air, although the scale in fact is small. The main body of the church is thirteenth-century and is fairly plain, except for a varied collection of windows of several dates. On the north wall of the chancel is a monument to Richard Ball, 'Pastor of this Parish', who died in 1632. He kneels on a green hassock with golden tassels and his priedieu is upholstered in the same attractive manner.

The Red Lion, which stands suitably below the church and beyond a little green, is a highly picturesque timber-framed building with overhanging upper storey. It is claimed that at least parts of it were built in the fifteenth century, but since this style of construction persisted for several centuries, it is hardly possible to date it very exactly.

Less than two miles south of Chalton along the narrow road running along the valley parallel to the railway one comes to one of the strangest, and in some ways one of the most interesting, little churches in the county. This is the Chapel of St Hubert at Old Idsworth. It stands isolated from all other buildings on a knoll on the east side of the road, and is approached by a long grass path which crosses the arable fields that surround it. Behind it runs a long range of wooded hills which are in fact in Sussex, and in front across the valley are bare, down-like slopes. A thoughtful notice at the gate at the foot of the path assures one that the chapel is always open.

It is built of the materials usual in this area of flint and stone with a tiny wooden bell turret at the junction of the nave and chancel. The nave is twelfth-century and the chancel dates from the following century. In the sixteenth century the former was widened on the south side so that the eighteenth-century entrance porch and chancel are now out of centre. Having been left derelict for many years it escaped nineteenth-century restoration, but was repaired with great care by H. S. Goodhart-Rendel in 1912. The coved plaster roof of the chancel with roundels set in rectangles formed by simulated cables is his work—perhaps an idea remotely borrowed from Robert Streater's painted ceiling at the Sheldonian Theatre at Oxford of 1664. The box pews, which fill the front part of the nave, and the Jacobean pulpit survive from the original furnishings.

But the feature which raises this little church into the highest category of interest is the wall paintings on the north wall of the chancel. These are thought to date from about 1320, and are divided by a painted band of decoration into two tiers. Above are apparently scenes from the life of St Hubert with horseman and hounds, and a strange creature half man, half animal whom the figure of the saint is curing from the belief, which seems well-founded, that he is a wolf. Below, the dominant figure is that of Salome doing a spirited sword dance before Herod and his friends, while the head of the saint is being handed up on a dish. There are traces of other murals on the east wall of the chancel, but they are so vague that even Professor Tristram failed to decipher them.

To the south of the knoll on which the chapel stands is the site of the old manor house, almost on the line of the railway which runs through the valley, and on the westward slope is a wide avenue of lime trees which was centred on the vanished house. The old house having been demolished in the cause of progress, an ambitious new Idsworth was erected from the designs of William Burn in 1852 on high ground a mile or so away to the south-west. The valley leads on southward to Rowlands Castle, a place less romantic than its name would suggest, and the agreeable sense of solitude and remoteness which we have been enjoying to the north vanishes as we reach the village.

CHAPTER SIX

The ports and southern seaboard

In the last chapter we kept carefully to the southern border of the chalk country, not even putting a delicate foot over the edge on to the long belt of clay and coarse sand known geologically as the Reading Beds, which runs in a long line roughly parallel to the coast of Spithead. We ended our peregrination of this eastern part of the county at Rowlands Castle, which is not only on the junction of these two soils but also on the eastern boundary of Hampshire with Sussex, so this seems a good point to start our advance westward, taking in Portsmouth and travelling up to Southampton, and as far as the banks of the river Test which pours its waters into Southampton Water between Redbridge and Totton. We will also examine the sadly overpopulated country which lies behind the two great ports. But if this is far from being the most attractive part of the county, particularly for those who like open country with little villages in folds of the hills, and a general scene of solitude, there is much interesting architecture to be found amongst the spread of building which is fast submerging the area.

Due west of Rowlands Castle is the area known as the Forest of Bere, which technically stretches away for eight miles or so towards the west, but it is a forest only in name; and, although there are still some large woodlands within its compass it bears no comparison with, for example, Alice Holt Forest, described in Chapter Five, where forestry is still actively carried on. But having once been nominated, like the New Forest, a forest area it thus remains in name if not in fact. The London–Portsmouth road, the A 3, passes through the nominal Forest, but, alas, more building is now to be seen along this unattractive, almost urban stretch of highway, than ancient forest land.

28 In Emsworth Harbour

However in 1807 the aspect was different, for in that year J. M. W. Turner passed through the Forest on his way to Portsmouth to watch the arrival of Stanhope's squadron, after the surrender of the Danish fleet at Copenhagen, and was so impressed by the aspect of the woodland in the golden October sunshine that it inspired him to one of his most attractive landscapes. It can now be seen at Petworth House.

Having now somewhat exploded the Forest of Bere, we will turn south towards the three shallow, almost landlocked harbours which make their rather surprising appearance on the smooth coastline of Spithead. Of these harbours two, Portsmouth and Langstone, are wholly in Hampshire, while the greater part of the third, Chichester, is credited to Sussex, the county boundary running up Emsworth Creek so that the Island of Hayling, which divides Chichester from Langstone, lies in Hampshire.

Just squeezing into Hampshire is the little town of Emsworth standing on the estuary of the Ems, a river of negligible size but affording an attractive site for the town, and in the past a useful harbour. For Emsworth was for centuries a thriving port served by ships which sailed through the sheltered channels of Chichester harbour to discharge their cargoes on its quays. It was still a prosperous place in the eighteenth century, as can be deduced from the many handsome houses of this period. In the last century, when trade left it, the place decayed, but it has now revived as a centre—and a charming one—of sailing. Thus commerce has given way to pleasure, and Emsworth is once again on the crest of the wave.

The original parish church of Emsworth was a mile to the west of the town at Warblington, and it is well worth turning southward out of the turmoil and bustle of the big new roads to visit it and the ruins of the castle which stand at the end of a quiet lane. There is now no village to justify a church, and it stands low and spreading, surrounded by tall trees and unspoiled meadows which extend to the channel which joins the harbours of Chichester and Langstone. The entrance is at the west end, and this façade presents a strange, almost triangular appearance, for the roofs covering the side aisles sweep down on either side to within a few feet of the ground. The

29 HMS *Victory*

greater part of the building dates from the late twelfth century and from the first quarter of the following, but part of the little tower which rises at the junction of nave and chancel is clearly pre-Conquest, and probably marks the west end of the original church, the chancel being on the site of the nave. The growth of the church is complex, but even without exact knowledge of dates, the charm of the building on its romantic site is extreme.

Little now remains to show the extent of Warblington Castle, but the tall surviving octagonal turret in brick and stone, which must have been part of the entrance gateway, shows that it was a place of considerable importance. Queen Elizabeth stayed for two days at Warblington during her progress through the southern counties in 1586, and it was no doubt on the Castle that she and her retinue descended. It was one of those excursions which proved exceedingly expensive for the owners of country houses, but which made agreeably little demand on the royal purse. The Castle was seriously damaged during the Civil War, and no attempt was made after that date to arrest decay.

To reach Hayling Island we turn southward in Havant, an expanding town where we need not delay, and so come to Langstone Village, a group of houses on the border of the wide channel, known as Sweare Deep, which separates the island from the mainland. Until two decades ago the only road across the water ran over a causeway and a long, narrow bridge supported on wooden piles. Until 1823 there was not even this rickety bridge, and the only way to cross the treacherous creek was by boat, so that during winter gales the island was often cut off for days from the mainland. Although the Regency bridge may have been adequate for farm carts and an occasional *calèche,* its narrowness, with the addition of a turnpike gate, became a nightmare for those trying to reach the island during summer weekends. Now the situation is vastly improved.

By the side of the old road bridge there was a railway bridge, in appearance equally fragile and insecure, which has been allowed to survive as a memorial of the past. On these shuddering supports a little train almost as antiquated apparently as the bridge would puff precariously back and forth from Havant Station to the southern part of the Island. The memory of this courageous machine is felicitously commemorated in the name of a new pub on the Island, The Hayling Billy, and a portrait of the engine forms the inn sign.

The Island has no particular beauty, but its flat fertile fields and sandy southern shore must have had an artless charm before it became a 'resort'. But nearly a century and a half ago the first developer invaded its tranquillity, and optimistically began the erection of a crescent of large houses on a stretch of open ground which borders the shore. Hayling, one imagines him saying to himself, will become another Brighton. But the enterprise was clearly a failure, for only half the crescent was ever built, and this genteel, urban group of tall houses, with basements and areas, looking as if a section of Bayswater had been transported to the seaside, remains as an uncomfortable memorial of an over-optimistic scheme.

About two thirds of the island is now covered by the roads and buildings inevitable to a pleasure resort. There is no particular centre, but houses and shops spread about in a desultory way over the whole of the southern section of the island. The north-east area, however, unexpectedly retains its simple pastoral character, and here serving the parish of North Hayling is the charming little church of St Peter. It dates principally from the twelfth and thirteenth centuries and consists of a nave with very narrow north and south aisles and arcades supported on sturdy columns. Three huge buttresses discourage the east end from falling out into the road.

South Hayling, just within the pleasure belt, also has a basically thirteenth-century church. It is larger and grander than its northern sister but, to me at least, is much less sympathetic. Both Street and Blomfield were at work here in the last century, and although their restorations were scholarly, the well-chiselled stonework gives the church a harsh appearance. However, the four wide Gothic arches at the crossing under the central tower are impressive. So also is a yew tree of immense antiquity near the south porch.

A channel only a few hundred yards in width separates the western point of Hayling with the eastern of Portsea Island, and a ferry battles through the strong tides of this narrow opening from point to point. But I propose to lead the reader round Langstone harbour by road so as not to miss the attractive little village of Bedhampton. I should perhaps confess that I have a special affection for the place, for I lived there from 1936 to 1938. Even then the village seemed threatened by surrounding development, and since that time new roads and buildings have almost engulfed it, but it has fortunately been allowed to keep its head just above water.

When I lived there, almost every house and cottage in the casual group of buildings was attractive. The Manor House, where I was, was not of any architectural importance: the central part of the house is early seventeenth-century, and the wings are Victorian, but the high brick wall which surrounds the garden with an arched door into the meadow is probably contemporary with the centre of the house. Beyond the wall stands the church, which is rather an essay in nineteenth-century restoration than a building of antiquity, but the chancel arch dates from the mid-twelfth century.

It is really the eighteenth-century houses scattered about which provide the charm, and of these the one known as The Elms on the west side of the village is particularly fascinating. In the late eighteenth century a Gothic Revival stucco front was added to an earlier body, and with its semi-Gothic, semi-Venetian windows it has an engagingly amateurish appearance.

South of Bedhampton and beyond the busy roads damp meadows—*prés salés*, since they are occasionally covered by the tide—fringe the great expanse of Langstone harbour. These silted harbours of mud and sea have a mournful charm of their own. Many thousands of acres of shallow, shimmering water are broken by the green and brown surfaces of the islands and banks which stand above the highest tides, and extend away to the barrier which divides the harbour from Spithead, and to the distant cranes and chimneys of Portsmouth which raise their fretted outline against a wide expanse of sky.

Richard Gough wrote of Langstone in his edition of *Britannia* of 1789: 'It is capable of containing the whole navy of England, but for the bar of sand across its mouth.' While in 1859 William White announced in his *Gazetteer* that it was then proposed 'to deepen the channel, to construct docks, and to convert this immense tidal basin into a capacious harbour for large ships'. Of late years there have been other ambitious schemes to make use of this great space, half sea half land, a seaplane base, an airport, and so forth, but so far none of these projects has materialised, and these desolate wastes are left to the enjoyment of the gulls and the flocks of swans which at times descend in quantities on these mud-girt waters.

Beyond the marshes a fine new road turns southward on to Portsea Island, for it is indeed an island although the Portsbridge Creek which separates it from the mainland is barely noticeable. This road skirts down the east side of the island, thus avoiding the tedious northern suburbs of Portsmouth, and arrives in the polite, seaside streets of Southsea. It is a place which needs no description, it is just jolly and salubrious, with terraces of nineteenth-century stucco houses facing across the grassy common to the sea, so let us continue into Old Portsmouth on the western side of the island.

This naval port was inevitably a particular target during the last war, and the damage it suffered was very severe. In the north part of the town, which consisted principally of singularly unbeautiful nineteenth-century development, the loss from the architectural angle was negligible, but in the old town which crowded within its walls close to the channel from Spithead to Portsmouth Harbour it was a different matter. There is little to be gained by moaning about beauties that have disappeared, but I feel bound to say that the Old High Street was until the war one of the most charming streets in the county. It still has charm, for it still sweeps down in a gentle curve to the great bastion wall, a surviving part of Henry VIII's defences, and the gilded bust of Charles I in its niche high on the wall still meets the eye as one descends the street. But the greater number of the seventeenth-, eighteenth-, and early nineteenth-century houses, which bordered the street and with their diverse styles gave it so much character, have disappeared.

There are a few, a very few, fortunate survivors. No. 60, at the corner of Grand Parade, dates from 1789, and has a rusticated and arcaded ground floor, while the house on the east side in which

George Villiers, Duke of Buckingham, was murdered by Felton in 1628 is another which escaped the bombs. The timber-framed building was refronted about 1700 and its interest is historical rather than architectural. The assassin Felton was executed at Tyburn, and his body was then brought back to Portsmouth and hung in chains on the beach. In St Thomas' church, now raised to the dignity of a cathedral, a very grand monument by Nicholas Stone was erected to the murdered duke by his sister, the Countess of Derby. In the house numbered 73, one of the war casualties, George Meredith, spent the first ten years of his life, his father carrying on here a business as a tailor. It was not, however, his birthplace.

The Cathedral stands on the north-west side of the Old High Street and was originally concealed from it by buildings, but is now opened to it, and this perhaps can be considered one of the few improvements created by bombing. It is a complex building of many dates from the twelfth century to the present day. The most attractive feature of the exterior is the late seventeenth-century tower in a simplified Wrenish style, and in the interior much twelfth-century work survives in the chancel and transepts. Shortly before the last war large additions were made, but not completed, from designs by Sir Charles Nicholson, and further enlargements in a contemporary style are now in progress.

The town was naturally well defended before Henry VIII came to the throne, but the ramparts were gradually reinforced as part of his scheme for defending the vulnerable parts of the south coast. Only the southern section still survives from the King's Bastion on the Southsea side to the Round Tower at the narrowest point of the channel to the harbour. For half the length the waters of Spithead still lap the walls, and with their height and robustness it is possible to appreciate how well-defended the place must have been in Tudor days.

The Dockyard lies within the harbour, and the public is allowed through its gates to visit HMS *Victory*. But no vague wandering is permitted, except on special occasions, such as Navy Week, when restrictions are less severe.

On 14 May 1662 the English fleet under the command of Lord

Sandwich sailed into Portsmouth bringing Charles II's bride, Catherine of Braganza, with her Portuguese and English train. But it was not till six days later that the King, who was delayed in London by Parliamentary work, arrived in the town after journeying all through the night. The Princess was slightly indisposed, or perhaps put out by Charles' lack of haste, and she received her future husband in bed. 'It was happy for the honour of the nation', wrote Charles to Clarendon next day, 'I was not put to the consummation of the marriage last night, for I was so sleepy, having slept but two hours on my journey, that I am afraid matters would have gone very sleepily.'

The following day the marriage took place. There was firstly a Roman Catholic ceremony held in private in Catherine's bedchamber, and this was followed by a public service, presumably in the church of St Thomas, now the Cathedral. The couple remained in Portsmouth for several days, before leaving for Windsor and Hampton Court, and one wonders where in Portsmouth they stayed. Certainly no obvious building has survived in the town. Eleven years later in 1673, when his tepid interest in Catherine had long since cooled, Charles created his mistress, Louise de Kéroualle, Duchess of Portsmouth with the subsidiary titles of Baroness Petersfield and Countess of Fareham. Could memories of his brief honeymoon have accounted for Hampshire being so favoured?

In the north part of the town at 383 Commercial Road, a somewhat dismal thoroughfare, is the birthplace of Charles Dickens. He was born in this little late eighteenth-century terrace house in 1812, and it is now preserved as a small museum. When he was two years old his parents moved to another house in the town and then to London, so that his connection with the building was distinctly short.

Immediately across the channel into Portsmouth Harbour is Gosport and its residential companion Alverstoke. About 1540 Leland visited the site of Gosport and describes it in his *Itinerary* as 'a little village of fisshar men by much hethy and feren ground'. But the strategic importance, sharing the guardianship of the entrance to the Harbour with Portsmouth, was already appreciated, for about the time that Leland was visiting the 'little village', a block house and some ramparts were built, and these were extended and strengthened in the following century.

The town has long since burst its bounds, and building of houses and factories spreads northward so that it is now more or less united with Fareham. Housing estates and naval establishments, HMS this and HMS that securely anchored to *terra firma*, have spread over the flat fields to the north and to the west of the town. Good agricultural land has been submerged by this flood, but there was little of scenic beauty here except the village of Rowner. At the latter place, however, the church of St Mary with its churchyard, and an ancient thatched cottage with a spinney of tall trees, has been allowed to survive and makes a surprising, and one hopes much appreciated, oasis of antiquity in the sprawl of building. Fairly drastic restoration took place in 1874, but a good deal of thirteenth-century work survives, and the general effect is very pleasing.

Since this little book is intended to lead readers to places of charm and beauty, I will not advocate a visit to Gosport. Only those particularly interested in Lord Palmerston's chain of forts would find much of interest here, for in this area there are a number to be seen, some mouldering away as Piranesi ruins, others put to present-day naval purposes. We shall shortly meet more of them, on the Portsdown Hills, when their date and purpose will be explained.

Alverstoke is a polite residential suburb of Gosport. It contains a large nineteenth-century church designed by Henry Woodyer and in the road passing beside it there are some old buildings including a timber-framed cottage showing that there was once here a village of antiquity. But Alverstoke has one feature of real architectural merit, and that is the Crescent on the south side of the town. It was begun in 1825, almost simultaneously with its far less attractive counterpart on Hayling Island, and although only a section of a crescent it is a complete composition. It has a central pillared portico with long colonnades of fluted Doric columns, with iron balconies above, extending to end pavilions; the whole is stuccoed and painted white. The houses looked out originally over the flat foreshore to the shingle beach of Stokes Bay; some buildings now intervene, but a high barricade of evergreens provides seclusion.

Roughly parallel with and a short way back from the northern shores of Portsmouth and Langstone Harbours are the Portsdown Hills, a long range of chalk downs which thrusts its way through the flat surrounding clay country. The ridge extends for about six miles, from Bedhampton in the east almost to Fareham in the west with one not very deep, and perhaps partly artificial break where the London road passes through it. On a high point towards the west end of the ridge stands a tall stone obelisk erected to the memory of Lord Nelson. The survivors of his fleet each subscribed two days' pay towards the monument, and this is indicated in the inscription: 'Consecrated to the Memory of Lord Viscount Nelson, by the zealous attachment of those who fought at Trafalgar, to perpetuate his triumph and their regret, 1805.'

Along the crest of the ridge are six of the massive brick forts built in 1860 by order of Lord Palmerston as a defence against possible invasion by the French. Their offensive side is thus to the north since it was from the land that attack was to be apprehended, and from this aspect they are so well concealed by earth and grass as to be practically invisible; from the south, however, the massive extent of the buildings is apparent.

Before the last war several of them were ruinous, and in at least one the dark and cavernous interior was given up to the domestic pursuit of mushroom growing, and probably less reputable pursuits as well, but with the outbreak of war, like old soldiers, those that were not too far decayed were put to various useful purposes. Now two of them, Fort Widley and Fort Southwick, remain in Service occupation and their extent has been largely increased by all manner of outbuildings which sprawl about the crest of the ridge, much to the detriment of its appearance. The inevitable building estates now lap like an encroaching sea against the foot of the southern slope, thus covering what William Cobbett reckoned the best cornland in the country. 'The land is excellent,' he wrote. 'The situation is good for manure. The spot is the earliest in the whole Kingdom.' However, Portsmouth, crowded on its island, had to expand, and the former cornfields were one of the obvious places.

In spite of the building estates below and the Service expansion above, the view from many points on the roads which pass along and over the ridge remains superb. To the north one can gaze out over a wide, thickly-wooded landscape which might make one believe that the Forest of Bere was indeed still a forest, so well is building concealed by trees. The landscape has the prosperous comfortable quality of a Victorian water-colour—well-grown trees, lush meadows and areas of woodland—it seems imperishable; but, alas, Portsmouth has designs on this area too, and who knows what its fate is to be.

Southward from the ridge the view is more unusual and more exciting, for one looks over the whole expanse of the two landlocked harbours of Langstone and Portsmouth. Let us hope the tide is high, for then the mud flats disappear and the harbours are vast sheets of water. Across the water, all the paraphernalia of the Dockyard can be seen with a haze of smoke covering the town behind it and very likely several warships lying near the entrance to the harbour in the deep channels which can just be descried between the ramparts. From the north shore of Portsmouth Harbour a peninsula juts out into the water, and on it stands a miraculous building, the keep and surrounding walls of Porchester Castle. Is it purely county pride that makes me think it one of the most romantic ruins in England? Anyhow we will now descend from our vantage point and inspect it.

Having survived the hazards of the coast road, the A 27, one takes a turning on to the spit of land on which stands the Castle. The first stretch of the road is not very promising, but as it turns eastward the buildings greatly improve, and there before one rises the great stone keep with its spreading walls and gates, still protected from intrusion by trees and water. In the third century the Romans created their Portus Magnus by building a rectangle of flint and rubble walls, ten feet thick and 20 feet high, enclosing an area of nine acres, and it is these walls with their hollow, D-shaped bastions which still survive. The walls have been patched and rebuilt in places, and six of the original 20 bastions have disappeared, but these massive ramparts are still splendid examples of the scale on which the Romans built their fortifications.

The castle remained much as the Romans had left it until early in the twelfth century, when a keep of great strength was built in the north-west corner and an inner bailey was enclosed round its base with a wall and a moat. About half a century later the keep was raised to its present impressive height. The next step was the erection in the fourteenth century against the Norman walls within the bailey of domestic buildings, consisting of a Great Hall with buttery and kitchen at the east end, and a Solar and other chambers at right angles on the other side backing on to the Roman wall. At the same time a rectangular tower was raised at the north-east corner of the bailey looking over the Roman wall towards the Portsdown Hills. The final addition came in the sixteenth century with the building of further domestic quarters on the east side of the bailey.

With the exception of the keep, the stout walls of which are little marked by the passage of eight centuries, the buildings within the Inner Bailey are largely ruined, but their original form is still evident. The ascent of the stair in the keep is arduous but rewarding. The interior is divided by floors, which are not original, into a number of rooms, and from these one can see the defensive design of the double walls, and also the hygienic sanitary arrangements of long shafts descending from garde-robes formed in the thickness of the walls to the moat at the base of the tower.

From the summit one can look out over the whole extent of the castle and on to the expanse of shallow water beyond the walls. On the green sward of the Outer Bailey Henry V in 1415 gathered his troops before the assault on the coast of France which led to the victory of Agincourt, the army marching out through the fourteenth-century Water Gate on the east side to take ship for Harfleur on the coast of Normandy. At one's feet are the roofless rooms to which Henry VIII and Anne Boleyn came in 1535, with Anne's decapitation only a year away, when they were said to have been 'very merry'; and in 1601 Queen Elizabeth came in the course of what was probably the last of her Progresses.

The fortifications are not the only buildings worth seeing at Porchester, for in the south-east corner of the Outer Bailey stands the Norman parish church. Few churches can have a more romantic setting, though this is inevitably somewhat marred by what appears to be a highly popular churchyard. The chancel of the church was shortened in the sixteenth century, and at the same time the south transept was demolished, but otherwise the walls of about 1133 still stand. They are the survivors of the priory which was founded here by Henry I but which was removed after little more than a decade of existence to a more tranquil site at Southwick beyond the Portsdown Hills. The two great features of the church are the splendid, and unspoiled, west front, and the arches of the crossing beneath the low tower, good examples of robust Norman construction.

I have probably expatiated too enthusiastically about Porchester, but its setting, the simple beauty of its buildings, and the many centuries of history which are incorporated in its walls seem to me to make it a place of very special importance. May it long stand aloof and inviolate above the surge of building which is covering so much of the neighbouring countryside.

Sobering down from these ecstasies, let us return to the coast road, the A 27, and follow it for two miles into Fareham. As one enters the town the road crosses a tidal estuary which has some charm. Three centuries ago it had not only charm but also use, for this estuary of the river Wallington, which in spite of its rather imposing name is no more than a stream with a course of a few miles before flowing into Portsmouth Harbour, provided a port which brought great prosperity to Fareham. In 1630 Sir John Coke, Principal Secretary of State, wrote of it:

> The river leading to Fareham within a mile of the town is an absolute good and safe place to moor ships and in all respects as convenient and safe a harbour as Chatham, £2,000 may be saved to the King in moorings and men.

In spite of this advice, it remained a purely commercial port, and now since the channels have silted there is barely draught for a rowing boat.

Those hurrying on through Fareham towards Southampton may be forgiven for supposing that the architectural beauties of the place are nominal: they would, however, be gravely mistaken. Take a turning northward into the old High Street, and one is in as delightful a street as any provincial town can show. Wide and gently curving, it is bordered by individual houses of many dates, from low-timbered buildings to slightly assertive early Victorian stucco, with a good sprinkling of eighteenth-century between the two. Several of the latter are excellent specimens of their period, but it is rather the overall effect, an effect of high provincial prosperity, which gives the street its special distinction. It should not be missed.

Before going further westward, we will turn back to look at two little places on the north side of the Portsdown ridge, Southwick and Boarhunt. I call them 'places', for though the first is definitely a village the latter is barely a hamlet. Entering Southwick from the west, one comes into the straight, rising slope of the village street with attractive little houses and cottages on either hand, and the village church with its rather pompous little tower closing the vista where the road turns southward to mount the slope of Portsdown and northward to wander away across the area which was once the Forest of Bere. The whole aspect of the place seems remote and feudal, with no unseemly intrusions to disturb its peace. How long will this survive?

The church is not remarkable for its antiquity for, as a tablet on the exterior states, it was rebuilt in 1566, but it is remarkable as an early and rare example of a post-Reformation Tudor church. The building was not entirely reconstructed from the ground, for some parts of the mediaeval walls have survived, and some of the features are re-used material from the demolished priory. But the charm of the church is in its interior, which was fortunate enough to escape misguided restoration. So until 1950 it remained as it had been left by the eighteenth century, with its full complement of box pews and three-decker pulpit, and, as I well remember, it was a perfect example of an unspoilt parish church. In 1950 the pews were found to be wormeaten beyond repair, and were replaced by pews of modern design, but nevertheless much of the interest of the church survives, and the handsome tomb of the builder, John Whyte, and his wife stands beneath a canopy between the chancel and the north chapel. The latter died in 1548 and the altar tomb is Gothic in character, but the canopy which John Whyte set up when rebuilding the church, and a year previous to his own death, is of clumsy but engaging Renaissance design.

On the north side of the church is the gate into Southwick Park, a long drive leading to the large, formidable classical house which was built in 1841. It is now a naval establishment, and has been so since 1940. It was here that the decision was made in June 1944 to delay the date of D Day by 24 hours in the hope of an improvement in the weather. The Priory which, as has been mentioned, was moved from within the Roman ramparts at Porchester about 1145, was resettled in the south-west corner of the park. Here Henry VI was married to Margaret of Anjou in 1445, and let us hope that this was a rare happy moment in a reign of almost unmitigated disaster. The Priory was partly demolished at the Dissolution and, as has been said, John Whyte conveyed useful features to his new church. Some of the surviving walls were incorporated in a domestic building, but this was later destroyed by fire and nothing of the Priory now remains above ground.

A mile or so west of Southwick in a stretch of unspoilt country—rare in this area—rising from the Wallington stream up the slope of the Portsdown ridge is the hamlet of Boarhunt, known to us Hampshire Hogs as 'Borunt'. The minute pre-Conquest church stands on the slope of the hill and its plain, little-altered interior must resemble many that existed in the county until the vigorous restorations of the last century took them in hand. The west door was one of the few contributions of that period, when the original north and south doorways were walled up. The narrow semi-circular chancel arch with elliptical sinkings on either side, presumably for side altars, gives character to the building. Almost the only embellishment to this austere little church is a monument on the north wall of the chancel. Only the initials of those it commemorates are carved on it, but there is also the date 1577, an early period for the graceful Renaissance design of pillars and pediments with which it is decorated. I find myself constantly referring to venerable yew trees in churchyards, but here near the east end of the church is one which must surely be among the most ancient in the country. It is now hollow, but very lively.

The country to the west of Southwick and Boarhunt is fairly rural, but as one nears the Meon valley at a distance of four or five miles sporadic building breaks out and pastoral beauty is gone. Just beyond the Meon, however, one comes to the little town, or perhaps large village is a better description, of Wickham, which is exceedingly attractive. It was the birthplace in 1324 of William of Wykeham, one of the most revered Hampshire figures, whose bones lie in his chantry in Winchester Cathedral. As if conscious of its historical celebrity, the place has developed on unexpectedly dignified and spacious lines. The Square is wide and open, and on either side are a number of mellow red-brick houses dating from the seventeenth and eighteenth centuries, while in a street leading down towards the river, which skirts the village, are several picturesque timber-framed cottages.

It is strange in this doomed countryside, for I assume it to be doomed to eventual disappearance beneath bricks and mortar, or perhaps nowadays beneath steel and concrete, that between main roads there are still quite large areas of unspoiled agricultural land. I would suggest, therefore, that in going to our next point of interest, which is the small town of Titchfield, we should go a short way north from Wickham up the A 333 and then take a small turning southward by which we shall pass through one of the relatively quiet pastoral areas and so approach Titchfield from the north, thus avoiding the noisy main road via Fareham.

Shortly before reaching the highway one sees on one's right the imposing ruins of Titchfield Abbey, or Place House as it came to be called when the conventual buildings were domesticated. It was founded in 1222 by a colony of White Canons, who having received marks of royal favour developed here a large and thriving establishment. At the Dissolution it suffered the fate of all other monasteries, and was given by a grateful monarch to his invaluable Lord Chancellor, Thomas Wriothesley, Earl of Southampton, who was in an enviable position for securing desirable loot at this period.

Wriothesley converted part of the buildings to domestic use and to this end built a tall turreted gatehouse into the long nave of the church giving access to the cloisters which became an inner courtyard, while the various Dorters and Fraters were converted to a more comfortable and domestic aspect. By 1542 the adaptation was complete, and the Lord Chancellor was provided with a suitably splendid house. In the latter part of the eighteenth century it fell into disrepair, and a great part of the materials, valuable stone in a country of bricks, was transported to a site on the estuary of the Wallington where a handsome classical house, Cams Hall, was erected. This fine building is now itself mouldering into ruin, but Wriothesley's four-towered gatehouse and much of the adjoining thirteenth-century walling still stands and, in public care, is a well-preserved and agreeably melancholy ruin.

After several generations of Wriothesley ownership, a moiety of the estate passed in the early eighteenth century in the right of his wife to the first Duke of Portland, who took Titchfield as his second title, and then apparently immediately disposed of his share of the manor.

The small town of Titchfield lies south of the Abbey beyond the A 27, a very busy road which passes in a wide sweep between the two and thus by-passes the narrow and twisting thoroughfares of the town. The outlying streets are indeed narrow, but the High Street, when one has negotiated the various turns and corners, is unexpectedly noble in proportion. In mediaeval times it was, no doubt, a market place, and this accounts for its spaciousness. As a street it has not the grandeur of the High Street at Fareham, which we have been lately admiring, where the bordering houses are more important, but in a manner of lesser prosperity it has great charm.

Out of the High Street a narrow way leads eastward to the church, the west tower of which forms a terminal feature and with its short shingled spire serves as a contrasting emphasis to the low horizontal lines of many of the ancient houses which line the road. The tower, indeed, is that part of the structure which is of the greatest importance, for the lower part at least, is exceedingly early and formed a ninth-century porch to the original nave. The latter was rebuilt in the thirteenth century and further additions were made in

30 *Portsmouth: in Bath Square*

the two following centuries, while in 1867 the north aisle was unhappily reconstructed.

But the most exciting object in the church is the magnificent Wriothesley monument in the south chapel. It was erected in 1594 and is the work of a Flemish refugee named Gerard Johnson. It commemorates the first Earl of Southampton and his wife with their son, the second Earl, who died in 1581, and their three figures lie on the monument guarded by four tall marble obelisks which rise at each corner of the tomb. On the side face of the tomb are carved female figures in prayer representing less important members of the family, and on the ends are elaborate coats of arms and eulogistic inscriptions. The whole is a splendid and unspoilt example of Elizabethan gusto, such as one seldom finds in a country church.

West of Titchfield the menace of expanding Southampton begins to become acute, with sporadic outbreaks of building and industry here and there, all awaiting no doubt to be amalgamated into a single unity. But before plunging into the heart of this great town, there are one or two places which are still worth looking at. One comes first to the estuary of the Hamble river, which is probably the most popular haven for small-boat sailing on the Hampshire coast; it remains picturesque with steep banks leading down to a broad expanse of water covered with small yachts and with boatbuilding yards on the brink.

Hamble once rivalled Portsmouth as a naval dockyard, and in the reign of William III two 80-gun warships are said to have been built here, and two of smaller size in the first decade of the nineteenth century. A wall monument in the much-restored church in the adjacent parish of Bursledon, to Philemon Ewer who died in 1750, records that he built 'seven large ships-of-war for his Majesty's service during the late war with France and Spain'. The estuary was also a favoured embarkation point during the Napoleonic Wars. Lord Moira's troops mustered here for the crossing to Ostend in 1794 when going to the assistance of the Duke of York, and six years later Sir Ralph Abercrombie set sail from these peaceful shores for the campaign which ended for him in victory and a fatal wound at Alexandria.

31 *Porchester Castle: the Keep*

The country lying between the estuaries of the Hamble and the Itchen is now little more than a suburban district of Southampton, but near the shore of the Solent and midway between the two river mouths there survives an oasis of trees and grass sward surrounding the ruins of Netley Abbey. The site was originally open to the coast, but now a road and the grounds of Netley Castle, a fantastic nineteenth-century Gothic pile, intervene, and the Abbey precincts are reduced to a wide lawn bounded by a horse-shoe belt of trees which insulates the loveliness of these grey stones from the strident tones of modern building.

The Abbey was begun in 1239. Building must have continued for a number of years, for it consisted of a large church with a cloister on the south side surrounded by the usual buildings, a large part of which still stand. As at Titchfield, Netley was domesticised after the Dissolution by the first Marquess of Winchester, who had obtained possession of it. In this form it survived until early in the eighteenth century, when the then owner, Sir Berkeley Lucy, sold the fabric to a builder of Southampton for demolition. The purchaser set about his nefarious enterprise, but by remarkable and appropriate good fortune, as he was at work on the west end of the church, the tracery of the great window fell and killed him. One regrets that Sir Berkeley was not with him. In any case the accident seems to have acted as a deterrent to further destruction, so that some of the fabric was allowed to survive.

The Hamble rises to the north of Botley and its short course winds through the heart of the strawberry-growing area, where the soil is rich but the landscape is not very interesting, and much of the architecture is even less than interesting. But Botley itself is an attractive red-brick town, which is given an air of consequence by the little porticoed market hall which forms the central feature of the wide principal street. It dates from 1848, though the turret dates from half a century later. The whole is a nice piece of Victorian classicism.

Botley will always be connected with the name of William Cobbett, who lived in a house now in the grounds of Botley Hill from 1804 until 1810, when he was prosecuted for an article attacking flogging in the Army, and was sentenced to two years' imprisonment and a fine of £1,000. His disappearance from the village must have been a great relief to the parish Rector, with whom Cobbett was in a state of constant and violent quarrel. However, Cobbett was not a man quickly to forget an enemy, and when he passed through Botley on an autumn day in 1826 time had not softened his feelings:

> I had not seen 'the Botley Parson' for several years, and I wished to have a look at him now, but could not get a sight of him, though we rode close before his house, at much about his breakfast time, and though we gave him the strongest of invitation, that could be expressed by hallooing, and by the cracking of whips.

One has sympathy for the Rector's discretion.

Before going further westward it will be rewarding to make a short expedition northward to Bishop's Waltham. It might be supposed that this little town should have been included in the description of the chalk country, but in fact it lies exactly at the foot of the chalk hills and marks the boundary with the clay area which sweeps along the southern seaboard.

The most attractive approach to Bishop's Waltham is from the north, where the road descends steeply from the heights of Stephen Castle Down and plunges into the narrow streets which lie on this side of the town. Of late years this entrance has been somewhat eased and simplified, but formerly, to those not knowing the place, it seemed as difficult as trying to drive into one of Vauban's forts. Like Titchfield, however, the difficulties once negotiated, the main street is reasonably wide, and at its south end broadens into spaciousness. At this point several roads meet and the junction is known as George Square. In this latter part, too, are a number of eighteenth-century buildings, of which the stucco-fronted rusticated bank at the south-east corner is a curious example. Until recently it housed Gunner's Bank, which long survived as one of the few privately owned banks in the country.

The name of the town indicates that it was once a place of importance owing to the presence of a palace of the Bishops of Winchester, and the ruins of this once vast building stand on the south side of the town. Little now survives of the architectural splendours which the palace presumably once possessed, and from this aspect there is not very much to see. Such walls as still stand are principally fifteenth-century in date, though they incorporate some of Henry de Blois' stone work of three centuries earlier, but the burning of the palace was so thoroughly carried out during the Civil War, and it was subsequently used as a convenient stone quarry for other buildings, that little beyond the shell of the north wing of the original vast structure survives.

Though there may be little physical beauty left in these mouldering rubble walls there is intense historical romance in the memory of the four centuries when it was the favourite palace of successive occupants of the See of Winchester, and the frequent resort of monarchs and princes of the Church. Henry II, William of Wykeham and William Waynflete dated their wills from Waltham, and Cardinal Beaufort bequeathed his 'blue bed of gold and damask at his palace at Waltham' to Queen Margaret, the wife of Henry VI. When Camden compiled his *Britannia* in 1607 the palace still had some years of existence before it, and he was able to describe it as 'a right ample and goodly maner place motid about'. It was then surrounded by a vast park which stretched away into Waltham Chase and the Forest of Bere, and so appealed to those monarchs (and also no doubt to those prelates) who were devoted to hunting. As one looks at the Chase now, with its thickly-clustered outcrops of scarlet brick housing, it is difficult to envisage Henry VIII crashing about it in pursuit of wild boar.

The church is well placed on high ground on the north side of the town, and the handsome west tower with its pepperpot turret shows up well from streets and roads on a lower level. The church is spacious, as befits a place of this size, and contains a certain amount of thirteenth-century work, but money was no doubt too freely available in the last century and restorations and renewals were excessively drastic. One very fine feature has, however, survived: the pulpit. This splendid affair, in oak with a canopy, and side panels carved with architectural designs in rather elementary Renaissance style, was presented to the church by Lancelot Andrews, Bishop of Winchester, in 1626.

We must now return to Botley and continue our way along a singularly unattractive road which runs just to the north of Southampton in order to introduce the reader to North Stoneham church. A road euphemistically named Stoneham Lane leads northward from the A 334 and soon reaches the church which stands on the edge of a devastated park once surrounding a now-demolished classical house. It is a curious area of rurality lying between busy roads running north and south, and the ever-expanding urbanisation of Southampton and Eastleigh pressing on its boundaries.

The church dates principally from the fifteenth century, and the handsome battlemented tower at the west end from the following century. The interior with nave, and north and south aisles but no separate chancel, is light and spacious and contains three diverse memorials. The earliest is a stone slab in front of the Sanctuary, which is carved with a double-headed eagle and records that it is 'The tomb of the confraternity of Slavonians AD 1491'. How and why a number of Dalmatian sailors should have been buried here is mysterious. The other two monuments are more easily explained. The first is a massive Jacobean affair to Sir Thomas Fleming, who died in 1613, and to his wife. Sir Thomas became Lord Chief Justice and had the congenial task of sentencing Guy Fawkes to death. He is portrayed in his scarlet robes, while his wife is in black, and both are propped rather uncomfortably on their elbows, so that they can survey the interior of the church instead of gazing only at the roof. On the tablet below them kneel their six sons and two daughters. More to my taste is a fine marble monument to the first Lord Hawke, the admiral who gained the victory over the French at Quiberon Bay in 1759. On the marble panel of the sarcophagus is carved a representation of the British fleet preparing for this successful engagement. Lord Hawke, who lived at Swathling in the parish, died in 1781.

From the tranquillity of the Stoneham oasis one can join the busy main road into Southampton at Basset, and so enter the town by

The Avenue. Few great expanding towns in this country have so attractive and leafy an approach as the London road into Southampton, indeed the only comparable one that I know is Coventry when entered from the south. At Southampton a Green Belt has been miraculously retained and the highway passes along the side of the Common, so that on this side unspoilt country appears to stretch away, while on the other side a wide belt of forest trees and hollies obscure the buildings which rise behind them.

Having passed pleasantly down The Avenue one comes with a sobering crash into the town, and there is little to please the eye until one reaches the Bar Gate which formed the north entrance to the original town. On the way one passes the vast spreading complex of the Civic Centre. It was built in the decade immediately previous to the last war, and at this point of time it is difficult to appraise its merits; but at least it contains, amongst much else, an admirable picture gallery. It does not quite reach the level of Liverpool, Manchester or Birmingham, or those at Oxford and Cambridge, but after these Southampton comes in the very first flight of provincial galleries.

Like Portsmouth, Southampton suffered very severely indeed during the last war; it is not only what was lost which is so tragic, but also what was hurriedly erected to fill the empty spaces which is distinctly saddening. Above Bar, as the street north of the Bar Gate is called, was anyhow a purely commercial area, and here there was little lost or gained, but the postwar buildings which form an oval round the Bar Gate seem woefully inadequate. It is easy to criticise, but less easy to suggest what style of structure would have made a successful setting for this magnificent gateway.

A mediaeval gate bereft of the walls which provided its purpose is inevitably a difficult object, and in a number of towns noble veterans have been isolated, as at Southampton, in the interests of traffic. Should it be possible for them to remain attached even on one side, like the Westgate at Winchester, they still seem partially to be fulfilling their purpose, and the effect is correspondingly better. Ancient Roman arches, or their eighteenth-century descendants, such as the Marble Arch in London or l'Arc du Carrousel in Paris, were designed to stand alone, or at most with an iron grille on either side, and do not suffer when standing in isolation.

The Southampton Bar Gate is a particularly fine example of a town gateway. The central arch dates from the end of the twelfth century, while the north side, which is the most spectacular, dates from about 1400. Other centuries have made their contribution, particularly, of course, the nineteenth, but nevertheless the structure forms a harmonious and handsome whole.

South of the Bar Gate a long street leads down to the quay on the edge of the water. Leland in his *Itinerary* of 1538 wrote in flattering terms of this, the principal street of the town, as: 'One of the fairest streates that ys yn any town of al England, and it is welle buildid for timbre building.' I well remember that before the war it was still a street of great charm, although the 'timbre building' had been replaced by genial late eighteenth- and early nineteenth-century façades. However, as at Portsmouth, little is to be gained by regretting what has gone. Let us hurry on and inspect the impressive town walls which fortunately still survive.

Dating basically from the thirteenth and fourteenth centuries, these formidable ramparts encircle with some intermissions much of the south of the old town and pass in a long sweep up the west side, with robust towers standing here and there. No doubt the water originally lapped the base of the walls, but now a road passes below them forming a quay. Walled towns are so rare in this country that one feels oneself already transported to the Continent as one surveys these strong defences. The impression is increased if one enters the little French Protestant church in Winkle Street, near God's House Tower at the south-east corner of the walls. It is not particularly remarkable for architectural merit, as only vestiges of the original twelfth- or early thirteenth-century stonework have survived, but the strangeness of this little building which has sheltered a foreign conventicle since 1567 is impressive. It is extremely well maintained.

On the west side of the old town Bugle Street, which still contains a number of old houses and also some well-designed new buildings, leads northward to St Michael's Square. On the west side of the

Square is the Tudor House Museum, an excellent example of a town house built somewhere about 1500. It stands high above the ramparts which here obviously surrounded a low cliff, so that the level of the ground within them forms a natural platform. It is a brick and timber-framed building. Drastic restoration in this century has given the exterior a rather spurious look, but the original form survives, and the Great Hall which is probably the earliest part of the building is distinctly fine.

Opposite Tudor House, on the east side of the Square, is St Michael's church, a fortunate survivor, with its tall and graceful spire, of bombardment. A small amount of Norman work still exists in the base of the tower, and there is fourteenth- and fifteenth-century building in the aisles and chapels, but the nineteenth century, both early and late, laid a heavy hand on it, and to me at least the interior is not very sympathetic. It contains, however, the fourth of the twelfth-century fonts, carved in Tournai marble, to be found in Hampshire, the other three of which have been described in earlier chapters.

In the foregoing paragraphs I have concentrated on the historical aspect of the town, but to many the most interesting and exciting spectacle in Southampton is the vast commercial docks which front Southampton Water on the south-west side of the modern town, the area known as the Ocean Terminal. Here the great liners can be seen awaiting departure for distant ports, with all the complicated paraphernalia of cranes and gantries. Southampton may have suffered sorely in its architectural aspect, but as a modern, spacious, bustling, prosperous town it has few equals in England.

32 *Titchfield church: the Southampton monument*

33 *Southampton: God's House Tower and Gateway*

34 *Southampton: Bargate*

CHAPTER SEVEN

The Isle of Wight

During the decades since the past war the Isle has undergone a marked change in character. In the old days—and my acquaintance with the island goes back more years than I like to remember—it was a place well designed for a peaceful holiday and propitious for quiet drives through the leafy lanes to the many sites of interest in which it abounds. No longer, however, is it possible to wander tranquilly amongst the grey stones of Carisbrooke Castle musing on the tragic fate of a misguided monarch, or to contemplate in solitary and tender melancholy—to use Jane Austen's words—the wild cliffs of Alum Bay.

The present situation is very different. From early spring until late autumn flocks of huge motor coaches trundle along the deep and often narrow roads and decant their cargo of sightseers at this or that place of scenic or architectural interest. The island, indeed, has become a 'People's Playground', and the authorities have adapted the place to this seasonal influx by creating, as is unavoidable, huge car and coach parks and the inevitable 'Toilets' at all points of vantage. The secluded charm of the Isle has, it must be admitted, disappeared for ever, but, as I have said elsewhere, it would be a mistake to lament too loudly, for the sum of pleasure now provided is infinitely greater than in the old days. Indisputably, however, the island is now a place for those who prefer crowds to solitude.

Transport from the mainland has, of course, improved immeasurably in order to cope with the floods of visitors. There are the usual routes, particularly for those with cars, from Portsmouth to Fishbourne, and Lymington to Yarmouth, but the quickest route is by hovercraft from Southampton to West Cowes, (reservation is essential). This strange amphibious contraption will be found parked at its little port close to the mouth of the Itchen; it rises majestically from the concrete, sidles down the slipway, and with a roar like a helicopter tears down Southampton Water, bumps across the Solent

33 *Southampton: God's House Tower and Gateway*
34 *Southampton: Bargate*

(paper bags are provided) and 20 minutes later is parked on the slipway at Cowes. It is a highly efficient and punctual service.

Before setting out on a perambulation I think I should indicate the physical characteristics of the Isle, for a slight knowledge of the geology explains the curious diversity of landscape which is found within so restricted an area. The island is neatly diamond-shaped, and between its extreme points is no more than 23 miles in length from east to west, and 14 miles in breadth from north to south. It might be expected that the scale of the landscape would be in keeping with the size of the island, and this is indeed the case in the northern half, but in the southern half, where the chalk downs rise to considerable heights, the contours take on grandeur and nobility, so that as one looks across the wide valleys to these magnificent rounded slopes one feels one could be in one of the large-scale counties of England.

Geologically the island is divided into two almost equal halves by the long irregular line of chalk downs which form a backbone across the length from Culver Cliff on the east to the Needles on the west. The northern section is subdivided into the two Liberties of East and West Medina by the river of that name which, rising in the southern section of the Isle, passes through a gap in the chalk downs and forms a wide estuary extending from near the centre of the island to the Solent. The low-lying, gently undulating country to the north of the downs has a soil of stiff clay, known technically as the Bembridge and Osborne Series, lightened in places by areas of loam and sand. This soil accounts for the intimate, rather cosy and well-timbered landscape found in this area. Where the clay approaches the chalk downs a succession of strata reach the surface in a perpendicular formation and, stretching across the island, emerge to view in the strangely coloured cliffs of Culver and Alum Bays.

South of the downs lies a fertile belt of upper greensand and gault, descending to a wide area of lower greensand through which rises the great block of chalk downs, the highest hills in the island, which fills the south-eastern section. In the Undercliff which extends below the precipitate face of the chalk and the sea between Dunnose and St Catherine's Point the upper greensand and gault re-emerge, and provide a variety of remarkable geological formations. This south-eastern seaboard is a warm and fairly sheltered area, and on the steep slopes facing the sunshine all manner of tender plants—camellias, fuchsias, myrtles, palms, and so forth—give an exotic and luxuriant air to the gardens.

In the south-western quarter of the Isle the landscape is very different. Although the soil is fertile and forms good agricultural land, it is austerely bleak, and the Atlantic gales sweep across the russet-coloured earth and slice the rare, stunted trees which stand against them into weird geometrical shapes. In its appearance this area might be many miles from the sheltered green meadows and gentle hills lying beyond the central ridge to the north.

Having now more or less surmounted the hurdle of geology, we are at liberty to pass on and examine the works of man. As a generalisation I would say boldly that very few of the towns and even fewer of the villages can be said to be really attractive. Of the former, Newport, West Cowes, and Yarmouth have definite qualities, but of the villages there seems hardly one that can be really admired except Mottistone. Godshill, I know, is much praised, but to me its self-conscious 'artyness' is far from attractive.

A misfortune for the island was that a great deal of building took place when architectural taste was at its lowest point, that is to say during the last three or four decades of the nineteenth century. The majority of the holiday towns on the coast developed at this period, and in these, as in the villages, can be seen occasional buildings of respectable antiquity jostled and almost submerged by crude structures of the period when the island, largely under Queen Victoria's aegis, achieved a sudden popularity.

But there is one feature of the villages for which they are outstanding, and this is their churches. Almost every village, even when no more than a mile or two from its neighbour, contains a parish church of interest and beauty. It is true that the nineteenth century laid a rather heavy hand on many, usually with unfortunate results, but so long as the original fabric was allowed to survive they are well worth visiting. Almost always, too, they are remarkably well maintained, and it is clear that the small communities which they serve must feel great pride in their parish churches.

On the supposition that we have arrived in the hovercraft at West Cowes this would seem a convenient place from which to embark on our perambulation of the island, and we will start by examining this little town. It is a place of character rather than of great beauty, and this arises, I think, from the fact that it is dedicated to an industry—the industry, of course, is all that has to do with yachting. Along the shores of the Medina are the boatyards, usually ringing with the sounds of hammering and alive with all the animation that accompanies this industry. A short way inland from the shore runs the main street of the town, gaining considerable picturesqueness from its narrowness and twists and turns, but of greater architectural charm are some of the small streets, such as Sun Hill, which run steeply up the slope behind it.

Where the boatyards end along the waterfront, a rather noble esplanade has been formed, bounded by a balustrade from which there is an admirable view of the many yachts and boats lying in these sheltered waters; while where the esplanade narrows to round the point, stands the Royal Yacht Squadron Club with its exclusive lawn. Behind the Squadron building a steep street leads up to an unexpected structure—a classical archway, erected probably near the year 1800. It leads in fact up steps into the garden of Northwood House, which was presented to the town in 1929, and now houses the Urban District Offices. This is an agreeable building, finely placed, and designed in a simple classical style. It dates largely from the third decade of the nineteenth century, but the dominant feature is a wing on the north side designed like a classical temple with a low dome, earlier in style than the main house, but seemingly later in construction. Within the wing is a circular entrance hall ringed by pillars and with a coffered ceiling mounting into the dome.

On the south side of the house, beyond the trees, rises the strange tower of St Mary's church. It was designed by John Nash, who was the architect of a number of buildings in the island, in 1816 and stands above the vault of the family which owned Northwood House. It is an ungraceful essay in the Grecian style. The church, at the west end of which the tower stands, was rebuilt in 1867. The exterior is in stone, the interior is in red, yellow and black brick with stone piers to the arcades; there is a lavish use of pitch-pine. It is not, I think, a very sympathetic structure. A brass in the church records that Dr Arnold, Headmaster of Rugby, was born in Cowes in 1795 and 'received into the church', in the former building, four years later.

Beyond the estuary of the Medina, and joined to West Cowes by a ferry, lies East Cowes. Like its more important neighbour, the waterfront of East Cowes is active with various works connected with boat building, but beyond this narrow fringe of industry the quiet, leafy roads stretching up the slope are purely residential. Where the low hill drops to the Solent stands Norris Castle, perhaps the most successful of the several sham castles that were built in the Isle. It was erected by James Wyatt in 1799 for Lord Henry Seymour, and is a product of an earlier and more patrician wave of building than that which created the seaside resorts in the second half of the nineteenth century. East Cowes Castle (now demolished), built by John Nash for his own occupation, was another good example of the romantic style, and there were a number of other sham castles, now either demolished or in decay, which the rich and the noble raised amongst the wooded slopes of this unfrequented island. Norris Castle, however, was always the largest and most dramatic of the group, and it is a rare survival of an architectural phase in the history of the Isle. The gardens can be visited on Sunday afternoons during the summer.

Barely a mile to the east of East Cowes lies the park surrounding Osborne House. It was in 1845 that Queen Victoria bought the estate of 1,000 acres in order to provide a quiet retreat for herself and her family. The existing eighteenth-century house was not very large, and it is said that it was demolished and that the present rambling structure was erected from the designs of Thomas Cubitt under the close supervision of the Prince Consort. This I find hard to believe, since the original structure is so clearly apparent. On the entrance side it peeps out between the tall Italianate campanile on the one side and the obviously nineteenth-century additions on the other. From the garden and in the interior the eighteenth-century lines are even more obvious. However, it is not a matter of much moment, but it must be owned that the entrance front is a completely chaotic composition. On the left the Durbar Hall is contained within a classical shell while on the right the vast rectangular addition built to house the royal retinue is masked by a two-storeyed arcade based on Palladio's Basilica at Vicenza.

But it is in the interior that the immense charm and interest of the place lies. The furnishings and decoration remain almost unchanged since the Queen died here on 22 January 1901, and probably no more perfect example of mid-Victorian taste exists in the country. To those who suppose that mid-nineteenth-century taste was dull and gloomy, Osborne will be a revelation, for all is brilliance and colour in paint, decoration, draperies and furnishings, and if the detail is far from refined, it has a robust and cheerful gaiety which is highly engaging. All this, however, dates from the years before the Prince Consort's death in 1861 in the happy years of the Queen's married life, and nothing was altered during the 40 sombre years of her widowhood.

Aesthetically the greater part of the furniture is monstrously ugly—heavy, overornate, and coarse, and it is constantly an interesting speculation as to why taste deteriorated to so advanced a degree in less than half a century. There are other features providing interesting speculation, for example the vast canvas on the upper part of the staircase representing some frolic in which Neptune was implicated, where the nudity of bosoms and buttocks is startling in a house such as this. No doubt it was an introduction of the Prince Consort's, for in his bathroom is another life-sized, and indeed dangerously amorous, scene painted by Gegenbauer in 1830. Almost every room has its special reminder of the Queen's life with, and without, the Prince. In her bedroom is the great mahogany bed, with its heavy half-tester, in which she died. The portrait and other mementoes of her husband are still on the table beside it, while the flowered chintz in which her own and the Prince's profiles are outlined in tendrils, covers much of the furniture.

It would be pleasant to gossip on about Osborne, but it is time to move along. Before, however, we leave the area of the scene created by Queen Victoria, we must visit the church at Whippingham which was built to the designs of A. J. Humbert, the infelicitous architect of Sandringham, but, as at Osborne, under the supervision of the Prince Consort. The chancel dates from 1854, and the Queen laid the foundation stone for the remainder in 1860. The site is charming, at the summit of a gentle grassy slope leading down to the Medina, but in this very English landscape the church strikes a somewhat unexpected and Teutonic note. Indeed the central tower with its five pinnacles might have been taken from an illustration to one of Grimm's fairy tales.

In the church there is much to remind one of Queen Victoria and her family. On the south side of the chancel is the chapel where the Queen worshipped, and it still contains her priedieu, while on the walls are tablets to several of her descendants. The finest feature of the interior is the bronze grille in the *Art Nouveau* style to the north chapel which was designed by Alfred Gilbert. Within are the tombs of members of the Battenberg family, Princess Beatrice, who married Prince Henry of Battenberg, having been Queen Victoria's youngest child.

From Whippingham the main road to Ryde runs through pretty but rather highly populated country in a south-easterly direction following roughly the line of the coast. It passes first through Woolton, a concentration of modern building; but a small road leads to the little church which shows the antiquity of the place, for much of the structure, of nave and chancel in one, is Norman, and the south doorway with engaged piers and dog-tooth decoration on the arch is a good example of the period.

In a wide valley beyond the Wootton Creek lie the two buildings of Quarr Abbey, the ancient and the modern. The latter was built by French Benedictines in 1908 amongst the trees on the west side of the valley. It is curious but effective, decorated in stripes of red and yellow brick which has mellowed little in the course of 60 years, and was designed by Dom Paul Bellot. The ancient abbey, which is also the property of the monastery, was founded by the Cistercians in 1131 and prospered until the Dissolution in 1539. The sparse ruins of this once-important house spread about the valley with lengths of grey stone walls, gay in spring with yellow and russet wallflowers, with a few fragments of traceried windows rising here and there about the meadows showing the vast extent of the original layout. But farming has now taken over where the monks led their secluded lives, and visitors are not particularly encouraged—nor indeed is there very much for any but the specialist to see.

It is not necessary here to devote much space to the holiday resorts of the island. In general their development coincided with the worst period of English architecture, when they expanded from little fishing villages into large and prosperous towns extending their crimson tentacles far into the green recesses of the countryside. Sandown, for example, consisted of no more than a collection of fishermen's huts until the middle of the nineteenth century; 25 years later, in company with its neighbours, it had fully earned the appellation of 'pleasure resort'. These disparaging animadversions refer, of course, only to the architecture—as places for a seaside holiday they may be perfectly agreeable.

Ryde, however, is partly an exception to my strictures of the other large towns in the eastern seaboard, since popularity came early, and the houses are predominantly stucco, dating from the late forties and fifties of the last century. They are built in terraces on a slope so steep that a villa even at a long distance from the sea can without a twinge of conscience, and with its attic windows in mind, be named Marine View.

South-east of Ryde beyond a stretch of high, open country lies the almost landlocked harbour of Brading. It is enclosed by gentle, wooded slopes, on the northern of which is the village of St Helens, with houses set round a wide green. In long-past centuries several attempts were made to convert this shallow harbour into farmland by holding back the salt water. The most determined enterprise was during the reign of James I, when at the prodigious cost of £7,000 a local landowner constructed an embankment to close the opening. The great structure was almost completed when an exceptionally high tide swept over it and destroyed it; Nature thus once again showing her contempt for the works of man. Since that disaster no one has been bold enough to challenge the supremacy of the sea, greatly, as it has turned out, to the benefit of Bembridge on the southern shore, which has become the foremost centre for small yachts in the island.

The village of Brading, or perhaps it should be called a little town, from which the harbour takes its name lies a couple of miles inland, at the eastern extremity of the long line of downs which forms a backbone across the island, but the parish once embraced the whole of the eastern point of the island and this accounts for the importance of the church. It stands well, with broad steps leading to the three arches beneath the western tower abutting on to the street. The interior is spacious, showing elements from the twelfth to the sixteenth centuries, but the principal interest of the building is the Oglander chapel on the south side of the chancel which contains some remarkable coloured monuments. The most curious is that to Sir John Oglander, who died in 1655. He is portrayed in full armour lying cross-legged on his tomb like a crusader, while his face showing below his basinet and ornamented with a large moustache has a very ferocious appearance. It is an unusual example of the revival of a taste for the mediaeval.

From the main street of Brading a road mounts westward and follows the long, windswept ridges of Brading and Arreton Downs, and provides from this elevation of over 400 feet the finest views to be found in the Island. To the north the eye is carried over a wooded and undulating landscape, agreeable but not grand, to the Solent and Spithead with the cranes and dockyards of Portsmouth and Gosport and the long line of coast leading to Southampton Water forming the horizon. South, the prospect is dramatically different. Here the scale of the country is grand and noble, but curiously bleak. A vast agricultural valley stretches away to the rotund masses of chalk downs which fill the south-east section of the Isle from St Boniface on the east, rising to nearly 800 feet to St Catherine of a slightly lesser elevation, forming the bastion where the line of coast turns north-west towards the Needles. It is not only the nature of the soil which accounts for the change in landscape between the north and the south, it is also the wind, for the south-west gales tear between the central ridge and the southern uplands and few trees seem tough enough to develop in face of the constant buffeting.

In folds of the slopes to the south of the central ridge of downs, and thus protected from the direct force of the winds are two villages, Newchurch and Arreton, both of which have parish churches worth visiting. At the former one is immediately surprised to find that so small and remote a hamlet should centre round so large a church, but, as at Brading, the reason is that the parish was once enormous. Until 1861, indeed, it stretched from sea to sea, from Ryde in the north to Ventnor in the south.

The church stands proudly on a rise above the watermeadows through which the stream of the Yar winds away round the foot of the downs to Brading Harbour. The entrance is beneath the south tower which was added to the existing twelfth-century structure in the fifteenth century, but was rebuilt with its curious weather-boarded upper section during the reign of George II. Almost every century from the twelfth to the nineteenth has made its contribution to the fabric, but the first and unfortunately the last are the most dominant. The nave remains largely of the twelfth, but it was given its cruciform shape by the addition of transepts in the following century. A handsome ornament of the church is the lectern in the form of a pelican with three young carved in wood and gilded. It was brought here from Frome church in Somerset and must date from the early eighteenth century. One wonders why Frome was so unwise as to part with it.

The village of Arreton lies at the west end of the down of the same name and contains both an interesting church and a picturesque manor house, which is open to the public, but the traditional group is somewhat disturbed by farm buildings which intervene between the two. We will call at the Manor first, as this stands on the slope above the church. It is miniature in scale with an attractive E-shaped front built in stone above which rise clusters of brick chimneys and dates basically from about 1600, though additions were made in 1812. It contains several simply-panelled rooms, but clearly not all is original, while the attics have been converted into a museum of dolls of many periods.

The church at the bottom of the slope can be reached by a footpath from the house, but by car it is necessary to return to the main road and make a wide sweep round to approach it from the south. The exterior is dominated by the handsome tower at the west end which dates from about 1480, and is now supported by a pair of vast buttresses reaching almost to the battlements. The nave is largely Norman, with a north aisle added about 1200. The general effect of the interior is rather austere, but a more genial note is struck by two charming monuments by Richard Westmacott to members of the Worsley-Holmes family. The first is to Sir Henry, who died in 1811, and the second to his successor in the baronetcy, who was drowned in a shipwreck three years later. The latter monument includes a dramatic representation of the disaster, with a despairing female figure. There is a third fine monument by J. Haskoll to the last baronet, who died in 1825, on which the widow clasps a classical urn and two children weep at her side.

In the churchyard is the grave of Elizabeth Wallbridge, the heroine of the early nineteenth-century romance by Legh Richmond, *The Dairyman's Daughter*. The author, who was curate of Brading, became a well-known evangelical preacher, and if his memory has now grown rather dim, it remains green at least in this secluded spot.

From these quiet inland villages we will now return to the highly populated south-eastern seaboard and follow the road which winds along near the coast below the vast hills we have observed from Brading and Arreton Downs. There is nothing, I think, that need be said about Sandown and Shanklin, though the latter boasts a highly picturesque Chine. They are holiday towns and well adapted to this profession. But at Bonchurch two or three miles further south down the coast there is the really sensational Landslip. Here the narrow formation of upper greensand and gault lying between the chalk hills and the sea has seemingly slid down towards the shore, leaving exposed the limestone cliffs above, while the soft, fertile soil below is thickly covered with trees. Narrow steps lead down amongst the ferns and gnarled trunks, which cling to the steep face of the rocks, to the woods on the undulations bordering the sea. Descent and ascent are distinctly for the energetic, and to many the dramatic view from the edge of the cliff over the rounded tops of the trees in the woodland at one's feet to the blue waters of the Channel beyond will be sufficiently rewarding.

In a house known as East Dene, now a hostel, Swinburne spent much of his boyhood, and there played with the two sons of Charles Dickens who stayed in the town in 1849. Swinburne always held the place in great affection, and he is there buried in the churchyard of St Boniface.

Bonchurch practically adjoins Ventnor, a considerable town built on a slope steeper, I would suppose, than supports any other town in England. The work entailed in forming terraces one above the other to accommodate rows of houses and engineering zigzag roads and steps to connect them must have been enormous, and, it must be owned, that architecturally it has not been very satisfactory. Little here dates from earlier than the second half of the nineteenth century, and much from far later, but as a sunny seaside town with a climate as mild as any in the country it has its advantages.

Having negotiated the perilous hairpin bends of the road which rises from the west end of the seafront one reaches a highway which runs with comparative directness along the Undercliff to St Lawrence. It is undoubtedly one of the most beautiful roads in the Isle. The conformation is as at Bonchurch; on the north side runs the long line of limestone cliffs which appears beyond the woodlands through which the road runs. To the south the land falls away towards the sea glimmering between the tree-trunks, in places where hedges surrounding the gardens of the houses, which are scattered about on these balmy slopes, allow a clear view.

North of the great bastion of chalk downs, of which the cliffs above the Undercliff form the southern face, the character of the country changes dramatically. This is no genial, sheltered area, but a wide, open landscape of rolling down-like hills and spacious arable fields broken by occasional drifts of woodland. In this rather austere country, near the village of Wroxall, stands the romantic ruin of Appledurcombe House, surrounded by a devastated park extending over the gentle slopes of the hills.

I first saw this building in 1947 when it had perhaps sunk to its nadir. It had been empty since 1909 when the Benedictines who had inhabited it for eight years left it for the new Abbey at Quarr, which has already been mentioned. Decay had set in and this had been hastened by the explosion of a landmine close to the structure in 1943, shattering every window and shaking the roof. It was impossible to conceive a scene of more intense melancholy. The superb classical stone façades still rose amidst the cedars, ilex and copper beeches of the tangled garden, but within the walls all was chaos and decay. Beams had rotted, floors had fallen, shutters flapped against the broken window-frames, while across each end of the Great Hall a graceful colonnade of mouldering scagliola porphyry pillars supported a gilded cornice. The condition of the house, far the finest in the Island, was desperate, and demolition became a probability; but in 1952 it passed into the care of the Ministry of Public Buildings and Works, who adopted the only feasible plan of removing the roof and internal floors and fittings (the scagliola pillars survive, protected from the weather by sheets of corrugated iron) and making good the walls so that it now stands a majestic, empty ruin. Some of the romance may have disappeared but at least the splendid architecture of the façades will survive.

The house was begun by Sir Robert Worsley about 1701, replacing a Tudor building, and work continued over many years, and indeed was still unfinished at the time of his death in 1748. Although the building accounts make no mention of the architect, it is clear from Sir Robert's correspondence that he was John James, of Greenwich, an associate of Sir Christopher Wren and Nicholas Hawksmoor. The design, with its pillars, pediments, niches and swags, has a highly baroque flavour—a style which James decried in his later years. It was not until 1773 that Sir Richard Worsley, a grandson of Sir Robert's cousin and heir, began the work of completing the house, adding somewhat to its extent and redecorating the interior; he also commissioned Capability Brown to replant the park. Following a sensational divorce action against his wife, in which he was awarded only one shilling damages, Sir Richard left England for several years but spent his time profitably in acquiring one of the finest collections of Greek marbles yet seen in England, and also the collection of gems belonging to Sir William Hamilton. These with many pictures were housed at Appledurcombe and formed what became known as the Museum Worsleianum. He had no children, and on his death the estate passed to a niece.

The property lies in the parish of Godshill, but the village of that name is two miles away in the north-west. It is generally regarded as the prettiest village in the Island, and so indeed it once was in its artless way, with stone and thatched cottages strung along the narrow, winding street. But it has become a professional beauty, and to me at least all charm has left it. It is now designed to entice the tourist, and almost every one of the simple cottages caters for this trade. There are tea shops and tea gardens *à gogo*, pottery and gift shops, a model village, an Old Smythe's Forge (should you wish to buy a couple of cartwheels for your garden gate, here is your opportunity) and many little places for acquiring mementoes and postcards.

Serene on its hill above all these commercial activities stands the church, with a prospect spread before it to the south-west across a wide valley to the rotund forms of Span and Wroxall Downs. The exterior of the church is dominated by the tall tower at the west end, fourteenth-century at its base with a stylish superstructure crowned with battlements and crockets dating from two centuries later. The interior is surprisingly light, with wide fifteenth-century arcades which extend without break from nave to chancel. The monuments are an impressive feature. The earliest is that to Sir John Leigh, who died in 1529, and to his wife, a canopied altar tomb between the chancel and the north chapel with full-length figures carved in alabaster. Their daughter married Sir James Worsley, and so brought the Appledurcombe estate into that family. The latter are commemorated on the north wall of the chancel kneeling at a priedieu.

In 1741 the north transept was converted into a Worsley chapel, and here is a magnificent classical monument to Sir Robert Worsley, the builder of Appledurcombe, and his brother Henry. On a sarcophagus set between engaged pillars and pilasters supporting a pediment stand the busts of the two brothers. The monument was erected by

Sir Robert during his lifetime to ensure that he was commemorated with proper dignity, leaving to his heirs the task of adding dates and a fulsome epitaph. This, however, was never done, and the two brothers gaze out into the church above a panel innocent of even so much as a name or date.

From this inland excursion we can turn southward to Niton and so join the main coast road which winds round the great bulk of St Catherine Down that rises above the village to a height of nearly 800 feet. From the highest point of the road there is a distant, but not very well-composed view over the low-lying open country extending to Freshwater Bay and to the ridge of chalk hills which end in the Needles. On the summit of the down stands a tall fourteenth-century tower designed as a lighthouse. The oratory to St Catherine, of which it originally formed part, has now disappeared, but this strange octagonal building, this ancient pharos, with stone walls five feet thick, stands firmly against the gales which whistle and moan through the narrow lancet windows opening in each face just below the extinguisher-shaped roof.

The bare rotundities of the downs have through the centuries suggested the enterprise of building a monument or an eye-catcher on their smooth summits, and several are still to be seen about the Island. An irresistible site was the long spur which projects in a northerly direction from St Catherine's Down into the arable valley, and on this noble elevation a certain Mr Hoy erected a tall stone pillar of admirable proportions to commemorate the visit of Alexander I of Russia to England in 1814. This solid compliment was slightly vitiated 46 years later by the placing of a tablet on the reverse side of the monument to the memory of the men of the Allied armies killed by the Russians during the Crimean War. There are still two vacant faces on the base of the column: the process of blast and counterblast might perhaps be advantageously continued.

The highway winding down from these uplands reaches the little village of Chale lying in the expanse of level ground which extends far along the south-western seaboard. On the west side of the village, with a view away along the coast, stands the church, small in scale but handsome, with a fifteenth-century battlemented tower with a higher stair turret attached. 'Visitors Welcome' a notice board graciously announces at the gate, but the warmth of the welcome is somewhat modified by the fact that the building is kept locked.

The long, level coast road is not interesting, and it is pleasanter to turn inland into the high undulating country which lies a mile or two back from the sea. Here are three villages, Shorwell, Brighstone, and Mottistone, with churches which are worth visiting. Of these the first has the largest and most impressive church. It consists of a nave and two aisles, all three of equal width and divided by arcades dating from the mid-fourteenth century. This curious plan arose from the fact that in the fourteenth century the church was one of dual personality, the north aisle being the vicarial church and the present nave the rectorial. Whether rival services were carried on simultaneously is not recorded. However, the building of a south aisle in the fifteenth century resolved the duality, and the rectorial church became the central nave. The interior contains many features of interest: there is much woodwork, some nineteenth-century but attractive, and the stone pulpit built into the north arcade is unusual and seems to date from the same period as the arcades. The fact that the church is largely lit by candles must lend great charm to the evening services.

Brighstone is less important and has suffered over-zealous mid-nineteenth-century restoration, but the sturdy fourteenth-century tower, surmounted by a short spire of 1720, has charm. The parish, too, has the distinction of having had several rectors who were later to gain eminence in the church. Bishop Thomas Ken, who is said to have written some of his famous hymns in the Rectory garden, was one of these, and Samuel Wilberforce, later Bishop of Winchester, was another.

As I have said earlier, there are not many villages in the Isle which have been successful in retaining their charm, but Mottistone is definitely one of the few. Although the east–west road passes through it and is much used by the inevitable coaches, the serenity of the little group of buildings survives. It consists of the church, a few small houses and cottages, and the long grey Manor House lying below the down which rises steeply behind it, with the whole en-

35 The Isle of Wight: Looking towards Freshwater from Blackgang Chine

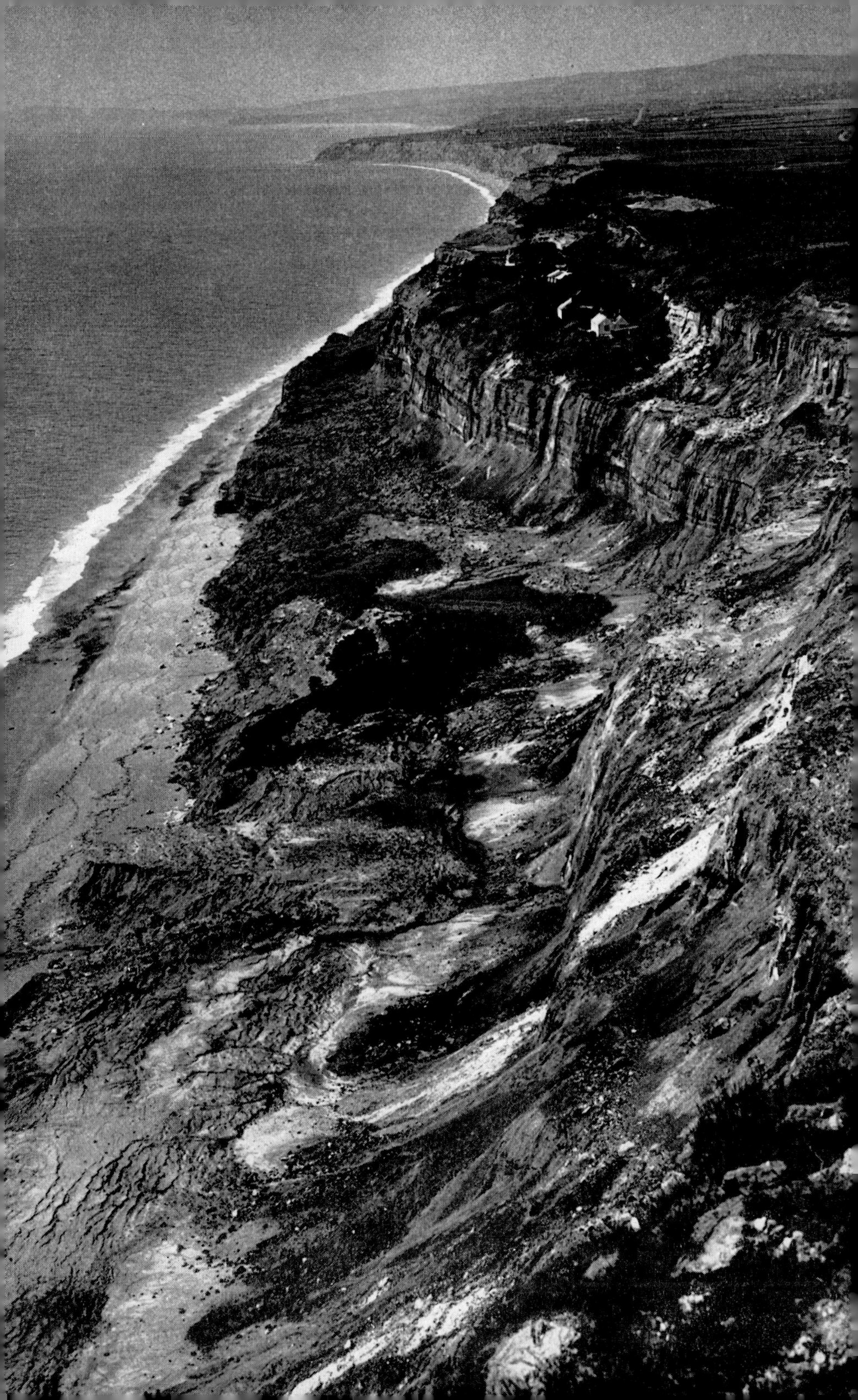

closed within a grove of woodland. The church stands on a rise to the south of the road. The fabric is basically fifteenth-century, but was much restored in the middle of the nineteenth; however, this drastic work has been carefully toned down by tactful eliminations during the past decades, and the general effect is now mellow and harmonious. Here, too, lighting is by candles, and this and Shorwell church must be two of the very few in the country to retain this beautiful form of illumination.

Moving westward, there is nothing to delay one till one reaches Freshwater Bay on the coast and the old town of Freshwater a mile inland standing at the head of the marshy estuary of the Yar, which more than half bisects the narrow western point of the island. The seaside town calls for no comment, but the old town boasts a church of considerable merit with a splendid west tower dating probably from the thirteenth century. We are now approaching the Tennyson country, for a mile to the west of Freshwater Bay is Farringford where he came to live, in quest of quiet and seclusion, in 1853. The house, now a hotel, is a long, low building with Gothic Revival windows and is partly stuccoed and partly in yellow brick. It is not particularly impressive, but the poet liked it, until crowds which came to visit him there became insupportable, and he wrote warmly of the place in a rather simple verse:

Where far from the noise and smoke of town
I watch the twilight brown
All round a careless-ordered garden,
Close to the ridge of a noble down.

The 'noble down' indeed is on its way to form the dramatic white cliffs which close the south side of Alum Bay at the extreme western end of the island. The road to the bay winds down between slopes golden in spring with the flowers of gorse, and has changed little in the past half century, so still remains much as I knew it as a child; but once on the edge of the cliffs all is altered, and catering for tourists has taken over with all the unlovely paraphernalia inevitable to the trade. But the prospect is eternal in its grandeur, with ice-blue chalk

36 *Godshill, Isle of Wight*

cliffs, shaded from the sun, dropping to the water and terminated by the jagged rocks so much more like giant teeth than needles, with a lighthouse on the furthest point; while at one's feet are the convulsed strata of various colours, ochre, bistre, grey and aubergine, which make this bay an inevitable objective for sightseers.

Fully to appreciate the strangeness of these formations, it is necessary to descend to the shingly shore, and this is now made possible, if not particularly easy, by long flights of wooden steps. On these tourists, ascending and descending like perspiring and panting angels on Jacob's ladder betwixt heaven and earth, dutifully 'do' this, one of the most noteworthy sights in the Island. When I was young glass *phalli*, intended to represent model lighthouses I suppose, filled with these coloured soils, were widely sold as mementoes of a visit to the Isle, but of recent years their popularity seems to have dwindled.

North-east of Alum Bay, beyond the much-developed Totland Bay, is Yarmouth, one of the most attractive and unspoilt little towns on the Island. It lies on the east shore of the wide estuary of the Yar, which forms as it opens into the Solent an admirable harbour for small boats. Approached across the bridge from the west side, the town groups agreeably beyond the wide waters, the clustering roofs dominated by the absurdly elongated tower of the church, while close to the shore looms the massive outline of the Castle, one of Henry VIII's chain of coastal defences.

The little square in the centre of the town, with the church at one end and the Castle at the other, contains all the principal buildings, including a charming brick Town Hall, of modest size, built in 1764. The church has been rebuilt and restored at many dates, and is not an impressive structure, but it contains a monument with a strange history. This is to Admiral Sir Robert Holmes, Governor of the Isle of Wight, who died in 1692, and it stands in a small chapel on the south side. By a piece of good fortune the Admiral captured a ship bound for France, and on board he found a sculptor accompanying a life-sized statue, completed except for the head, destined to represent Louis XIV. Holmes brought both the artist and his work to land, and compelled him to complete the statue with his own homely features. There Sir Robert now appears, his head, which seems a little oversize, topped with a nice plumed hat, while in his hand he holds a rather rudimentary telescope, but which for the King would, no doubt, have been a marshal's baton.

For those who find interest in unsuccessful enterprises it is worthwhile turning north from the main east–west road, near Shalfleet, where the church has a splendid Norman tower, to Newtown. The place was founded in 1255 by Aymer de Valence, Bishop of Winchester, on an arm of one of the creeks, now mostly marshland, which here break through the low north coast of the Island. The place prospered with the centuries and became a borough of some importance with a mayor and burgesses, and until the Reform Act of 1832 it returned two Members to Parliament. But long before this date, trade and prosperity had faded and the 'town' was little more than it is now, a few cottages scattered along a grid plan of narrow roads—and green lanes—a small Gothic Revival church built in 1835, and the Town Hall. This building, now the property of the National Trust, is the first object to meet one's eye as one approaches the hamlet. It was built in 1699, a charming little classical structure in brick above a stone ground floor, and with a wooden colonnade across the north end. Here the mayor and the burgesses carried on their phantom tasks.

Before entering Newport, the capital of the Island, one must visit Carisbrooke—not for the sake of the town, which, except for the church, is about as beautiful as Aldershot, but for the Castle on the south-east side. The position is impressive, for it stands on a circular hill rising in a gap in the long ridge of uplands which stretches from side to side of the Island, and dominates the valley formed by the river Medina which rises at the foot of the downs in the far south of the Isle. It was an obvious strongpoint, and on the summit of the slope, defended by a dry moat of tremendous depth, the Normans built their circular curtain wall, with a keep on an artificial knoll on the north-east side.

It is not the function of a guide—and that is what I am attempting to be—to discourage sightseeing, but perhaps I may be allowed to say that I find the crowds which throng the Castle a trifle disconcerting. On the other hand, these stout grey walls are splendidly preserved and maintained, and undoubtedly the Castle is one of the most interesting and picturesque fortified buildings in Britain. So let us take heart and cross the bridge over the moat to the magnificent fourteenth-century gatehouse and join the queue for tickets. This achieved, we may with luck get into the Chapel of St Nicholas, which is not very popular or indeed very ancient, as it was rebuilt during the first years of this century, but is by no means unattractive.

Thence we pass along the side of the courtyard to the building which attracts the greatest crowds of all, the Well House. Here the donkey trundles round in the wooden wheel performing a task quite useless except to amuse the public. You can, of course, buy a picture postcard of this survival, and so save a lot of waiting. To the north of the Well House and extending along the north Curtain Wall are the domestic buildings, which date principally from the last decade of the sixteenth century and form a picturesque group. They incorporate the Great Hall, the walls of which date from the end of the twelfth century but into which a floor was introduced in order to provide further accommodation at the time of the Elizabethan rebuilding.

The Hall now houses a museum on its two floors. 'No Smoking, no Dogs, no Prams' warns a notice at the door, so if you have not already mislaid your pram in the crowds you must park it as best you can. On the ground floor are well-displayed examples of Palaeolithic and later objects found in the neighbourhood; while on the floor above, which is reached by a charming stair dating from about 1700, are exhibits of rather more immediate interest. These are mementoes of the two male figures—Queen Victoria is of course the female—whose names are most closely associated with the Isle: Charles I and Lord Tennyson.

The King's stay in the Castle is one of the most melancholy interludes in history. In 1647 he escaped from Hampton Court, where he had been kept a prisoner, and made his way to the Island, where the sentiments of the inhabitants were largely Royalist and from which a flight to France in case of necessity may have appeared more feasible than from other places on the south coast. Moreover Colonel Hammond, the Governor of the Island who lived at Carisbrooke, was the brother of the King's Chaplain and might be expected to aid the royal fugitive. These hopes, however, were not fulfilled, and the King found himself as closely captive as he had been at Hampton Court. Two rather bungling attempts to rescue him were made—organisers of royal escapes are inclined to be inept—and on 6 September 1648 he was taken from the Castle to the Grammar School at Newport, not so much for added security but so that he could be present at the meetings of the Commission which had been appointed by Parliament to arrange a treaty with him. After two months of fruitless discussion, the King started out on the journey to London and to his execution.

The connection of Carisbrooke with this unfortunate family did not end here, for in August 1650 Henry, Duke of Gloucester, and Princess Elizabeth, aged 13, were brought there. The Princess died within a month of her arrival and was buried in Newport church, but her brother was kept here for a further two and a half years, and was then sent to his sister the Princess of Orange in Flanders.

The relics of the King which are here preserved are few—the nightcap he wore the night before his execution (a neat affair of white linen and crochet lace), and also part of the cravat of very fine lace which he wore on the scaffold. There is also a lock of his hair presented by Queen Victoria. The relics of the poet are rather more solid and mundane: his writing table, clay pipes, and other everyday odds and ends, and in addition there is his black cloak and large felt hat. How this massive sombrero was secured to his head in this windy island is a puzzle. Perhaps a store was kept to replace those that sailed away on the south-west gales.

The unlovely town of Carisbrooke now merges into Newport, which is very different in character. As is suitable to its position as capital of the isle it has considerable dignity and an unselfconscious charm. If there are few buildings of great distinction, the variety of their elevations with each house differing determinedly from its neighbour lends interest and picturesqueness to the streets. In the High Street, at about the central point of the town, stands the Town Hall, built to the designs of John Nash in 1816. It is a handsome, clean-lined, stucco structure with a noble portico supported on Ionic columns—too clean-lined for the Victorians apparently, for in 1887 a singularly inappropriate tower was added on the right-hand side of the façade.

There was no doubt once an ancient church in the town, but if so it was entirely demolished to make way for the present building, of which the Prince Consort laid the foundation stone on 22 August 1854. However, a fine monument to Sir Edward Horsey, who died in 1582, survives the rebuilding. It is a handsome affair with the recumbent figure in alabaster in a Renaissance setting of coloured marble. But the monument which naturally excites the greatest interest is that to the unfortunate Princess Elizabeth, just mentioned, which was set here by Queen Victoria in 1856. It is the work of Baron Marochetti and represents the child lying asleep with her head resting on an open book. It is extremely moving without sinking into sentimentality, the fault of many nineteenth-century child monuments.

From Newport the main road to Cowes runs almost due northward along the west flank of the valley of the Medina. A mile from the town it passes the buildings of Parkhurst Prison. The nineteenth-century elevation is unexpectedly genial for a top-security gaol, and has none of that menacing air which was so endemic a feature of eighteenth- and early nineteenth-century prisons such as Newgate and Pentonville. The more formidable parts of the building are no doubt kept out of sight of the public.

For centuries the long, wide estuary of the Medina was a busy waterway carrying shipping from Cowes on the coast to Newport in the heart of the Isle. In 1789, when Gough republished Camden's *Britannia*, it still fulfilled this important function, and in order to embellish the original description he added a translation, of rather dubious felicity, of the Latin verses composed in the seventeenth century by Leland about the locality:

Here the two Cowes that in loud thunder roar
This on the Western, that on the Eastern shore,
Where Newport enters stately Wight.

Index

The numerals in **bold** type refer to the figure numbers of the illustrations

Index

Index

Index

Index

Index